The
World of Ballet
and Dance

The World of Ballet and Dance

photographs by
Mike Davis
text by Fernau Hall

Hamlyn
London·New York·Sydney·Toronto

Published by
THE HAMLYN PUBLISHING
GROUP LIMITED
LONDON · NEW YORK
SYDNEY · TORONTO
Hamlyn House, Feltham, Middlesex,
England
© Copyright The Hamlyn Publishing
Group Limited 1970
Phototypeset in England by Filmtype
Services, Scarborough
Printed in Italy by Arnoldo Mondadori
Editore, Verona
ISBN 0 600 03980 3

*Front jacket picture Maria Koppers in the
title role of Fokine's 'The Firebird'
(National Ballet of the Netherlands).*

*Back jacket picture Ritha Devi in an
Indian classical dance 'Ahalya'.
(Odissai style).*

*Front and back endpapers, half-title and
title spread Josette Amiel and Jean-Pierre
Bonnefous of the Paris Opéra in rehearsal.*

Contents

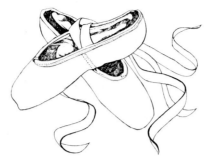

The Diaghilev Heritage

When Diaghilev began to bring his 'Ballets-Russes' to the cities of western Europe just before the First World War, the impact was overwhelming.

The Diaghilev seasons re-established ballet as a major art-form, and after his death in 1929 led to the setting-up of ballet companies all over the world.

A renaissance had been in progress in Russia for a long time before Diaghilev moved into the ballet world: ever since 1875, in fact, when Tchaikovsky was commissioned by his friend Beguichev, the Intendant of the Bolshoi Theatre in Moscow, to write the score for the first version of 'Swan Lake'. This ballet did not enjoy much success when it was produced in Moscow for the dancing and choreography were unworthy of the music and the libretto; but musically it was a major breakthrough, leading in due course to the presentation of the first great Russian ballet in St Petersburg. The renaissance continued right through the last decades of the nineteenth century, with each of its elements in turn (dancing, décor, choreography and so on) reaching a high level of artistry and technical skill. By the early years of the twentieth century further progress was difficult, if not impossible, for the Imperial Theatres were then run by men of little vision, and the more creative artists found their inspiration frustrated. Diaghilev revived the best they had done for performance outside Russia, and was soon commissioning new works like 'The Firebird', 'Petrushka', 'L'Après-midi d'un Faune', and 'The Rite of Spring': ballets which could never have been staged or even imagined for production at the Imperial Theatres. They represented a great outburst of creative energy, made possible by the organizing genius of Diaghilev: it was as if an atomic pile, given the right conditions, had suddenly 'gone critical'. The repercussions of this great outburst are still

very much to be felt today. After the Russian Revolution in 1917 a number of leading dancers left Russia, and many of them joined Diaghilev; but this source of supply almost completely dried up, and though Diaghilev was able to take on a few Slav dancers from Poland, he was still hard pressed, and replenished his company with dancers from western European countries, above all from England. By this time the art of ballet was generally considered to be necessarily and inevitably Russian; it was hardly conceivable that anyone with a non-Russian name could be any good, and so the dancers joining the company adopted Russian-sounding names.

The first of these neo-Russians was Hilda Munnings, an English dancer who joined Diaghilev in 1913 as Lydia Sokolova, and in due course (completely Russianized) became his principal character dancer. She remained faithful to Diaghilev right up to his death, and then returned to London, where her teaching made an important contribution to English ballet.

There were three other important dancers from England who joined Diaghilev. First, there was Patrick Healey-Kay, who took the name Anton Dolin when he joined Diaghilev in 1921. At first he took small parts, but he had developed some amusing acrobatic tricks which were perfectly in tune with the type of ballet that Diaghilev was producing at the time, and in fact Diaghilev arranged for Dolin to use these in the major role of Le Beau Gosse in 'Le Train Bleu'. Dolin later danced many other important roles including some severely classical ones, such as that of the Blue Bird in 'Aurora's Wedding' (Diaghilev's version of Act III of 'The Sleeping Beauty'). He danced this pas de deux with Alice Marks, who joined Diaghilev in 1924 under the name Alicia Markova. She was then only thirteen – the first of

Opposite page Marie Rambert in 1931, in Massine's 'Snegourotchka' ('The Snow Maiden').

Above Tamara Karsavina in 1912, in the title role of Fokine's 'The Firebird' (Diaghilev Ballet).

the 'baby ballerinas'. A leading role was created for her in 'Le Rossignol', and she stayed with Diaghilev up to his death. Then there was Irish-born Idris Stannus, whose stage name was Ninette de Valois; she danced with Diaghilev during the period 1923-6. All three of these dancers played important roles in the rise of English ballet.

Astafieva, one of the great Russian dancers, performed with Diaghilev in 1909-11 and then settled in London, where her teaching was influential in the development of English classical dancing: her pupils included such artists as Dolin, Markova and Margot Fonteyn. Other great Diaghilev dancers to settle in London were Karsavina, Lopoukhova and Idzikowski. Two great teachers who played major roles in the Russian renaissance and later worked as teachers for Diaghilev – the Italian Enrico Cecchetti

and the Russian Nicholas Legat, chief architect of the Russian school – also went to live and teach in England, and they helped in the attainment of a high standard of classical dancing.

Karsavina's invaluable contribution to the development of ballet in Britain was in coaching ballerinas for the leading roles in the classical and Fokine ballets, and also in helping to stage these ballets: the mime scenes that she contributed to the Royal Ballet's productions of 'Giselle' and 'La Fille Mal Gardée' did much to rescue ballet's great tradition of conventional mime, by showing that a dancer can use the formal gestures with the same spontaneity and emotional expressiveness with which an actor uses words (or an Indian dancer the conventional gestures called *mudras*).

Marie Rambert became associated with the Diaghilev company in its

golden age while she was working with Nijinsky on the musical aspects of 'The Rite of Spring'. She settled in London and formed the first British ballet company of modern times, thus initiating a renaissance in British ballet.

A number of Diaghilev choreographers and dancers settled in the United States in the twenties and thirties: among them Fokine, Nijinska, Vilzak, Shollar and Vladimiroff. They made the United States a great centre of classical ballet training, and laid the basis for the later achievements of American ballet.

George Balanchine, the Russian dancer who became Diaghilev's principal choreographer in the last years of the company, settled in the United States in 1935 and became the dominant force in American ballet after 1949.

A generation or so after the ex-Diaghilevians had established strong national

traditions in Britain and the United States, a number of British and American artists spread out in a second wave of dispersion and helped to establish national ballets in various other countries.

Something very like the complex pattern of decline, renaissance and dispersion to be seen in the ballet world in the last hundred years was also to be seen in the East, in Indian classical dancing, and this pattern of Eastern development had great influence on the ballet and modern dance of the West.

There has also been a pattern of dispersion in theatricalized national dance: in this case the general idea was developed by one man in one country (Moiseyev in the Soviet Union) and spread all over the world; it was applied in a great variety of ways, under the influence of ballet, or modern dance, or both.

Britain

ROYAL BALLET

Ninette de Valois

Soon after leaving Diaghilev Ninette de Valois started a school in London, seeing this as an essential step towards forming a ballet company and producing ballets on her own. In 1928 she began to stage annual performances of ballet for Lilian Baylis at the Old Vic, and when the latter had the Sadler's Wells Theatre reconstructed in 1931 she invited Ninette de Valois to form a ballet company to perform at both the Old Vic and Sadler's Wells (later exclusively at the Wells), an invitation of critical importance. The Vic-Wells Ballet was in fact established as only one part of a large organization which included a drama company (playing Shakespeare) and an opera company performing opera in English: all at cheap prices in theatres well outside the West End.

The standard of choreography and dancing of the Vic-Wells ballet in the thirties was erratic, but at its best it was very creditable. Ninette de Valois created some impressive new ballets: although 'Job' (1931) had its longueurs, it had a magnificent barefoot dance, much influenced by modern dance, in which Anton Dolin (as Satan) hurled himself over a flight of steps; and in 1935 Ninette de Valois choreographed her masterpiece, 'The Rake's Progress'. This was based on a series of prints by Hogarth, which it reproduced in groupings of dancers, décor and costumes. The climax was reached in a magnificent barefoot dance, in semi-modern dance style, in which the Rake, gone mad and sent to Bedlam, tried to push behind him his terrifying fancies.

Alongside her own ballets Ninette de Valois began in 1933 to commission ballets from Frederick Ashton, in a neo-classical style contrasting strongly with her own; and she gave the repertoire a solid basis in the classics by commissioning from Nicolas Sergueyev, who had for many years been régisseur-général of the Maryinsky in St Petersburg, productions of 'Coppélia' (1933), 'Swan Lake' and the 'Nutcracker' (1934), 'Giselle' (1937) and 'The Sleeping Beauty' (1939). In retrospect this policy seems an obvious one, for these ballets are now at the centre of the repertoires of national ballets all over the world; but it was by no means obvious at the time. In fact Ninette de Valois did great service to the art of ballet by getting reasonably faithful versions of these ballets into the repertoire while Sergueyev was still alive, and thus helping to preserve them for posterity. She also did well to take into her repertoire some valuable Fokine ballets–notably 'Les Sylphides', 'Carnaval' and 'Le Spectre de la Rose.'

In the early years of the company its leading dancers were the Anglo-Diaghilevian stars: Markova and Dolin. But Dolin was very much of an individualist, and never stayed for long in the company, preferring also to dance in revue and variety. Markova, in contrast, became the company's permanent prima ballerina, taking on the leading classical roles as well as new roles; but she left in 1935 to join the Markova-Dolin Ballet.

Fortunately Ninette de Valois had by then a number of other fine dancers–notably Pearl Argyle and Harold Turner from the Rambert company, Robert Helpmann from Australia, and two remarkable young Russian-trained English dancers, June Brae and Margot Fonteyn. All these artists developed rapidly, and Fonteyn showed outstanding promise when in 1937, at the age of seventeen, she took over the role of Giselle. Technically and artistically she was still immature, but she was already a great artist.

One of the strangest paradoxes of life in Britain during the Second World War was that the performing arts flourished as they had not done for centuries, in spite of austerity, mobilization of resources for the war effort and the ab-

Previous page below Frederick Ashton's 'La Fille Mal Gardée' with David Blair as Colas (Royal Ballet).

Previous page above Frederick Ashton and Bronislava Nijinska on the stage at Covent Garden at the première of the revival of Nijinska's 'Les Biches', with Deanne Bergsma (Royal Ballet).

Right Ninette de Valois' 'The Rake's Progress' with Robert Helpmann as the Rake in Scene 1 (Revival at Covent Garden after the War by Sadler's Wells Ballet).

Opposite Fokine's 'Les Sylphides' performed by the Sadler's Wells Theatre Ballet c. 1955, with Donald Macleary and (l to r) Susan Alexander, Ann Heaton and Margot Fonteyn.

sorption of millions of men by the forces. This was above all true of ballet: helped by government support, the Sadler's Wells Ballet, as it was now called, toured the country, and also appeared for regular seasons in the West End. It now gave far more performances per year than before, to much bigger audiences; and the standard went up, even though few new works could be staged, and the shortage of male dancers was often acute.

After the War the company found itself in an unusual and stimulating position when it was invited to come to the Royal Opera House, Covent Garden (now being established as a home for state-subsidized national opera and ballet), with help from the newly formed Arts Council. There was no suitable opera company in existence, and in fact the ballet company (appropriately enlarged) gave performances every night with enormous success. A new era had dawned for the company. All its male dancers had returned from the wars, and it presented a remarkable new ballet by Ashton, 'Symphonic Variations', as well as revivals of two ballets Massine had created for Diaghilev ('La Boutique Fantasque' and 'The Three-Cornered Hat'). By this time the Sadler's Wells Ballet had established itself as one of the world's finest large-scale companies, its only rivals being the Kirov and Bolshoi companies in Russia and Ballet Theater in America. When opera performances began at Covent Garden the opera company shared the week equally with the

ballet company–something unique in the world, outside the Soviet Union. This arrangement seemed to make good sense at the time, but it did not provide any scope for future development. Within a few years it was holding the company back, preventing it from giving proper chances to its leading dancers or satisfying the demand for tickets: in fact what the company needed was a share in two auditoriums, like the Royal Danish Ballet. A second auditorium was recommended by a committee set up by the Arts Council to look into the state of opera and ballet in the UK: when the second auditorium is available, the Royal Ballet will be in a strong position, able to perform every night and stage far more ballets.

Ninette de Valois ceased to create ballets after the War. With Ashton remaining as chief choreographer, she commissioned a variety of new works from other British choreographers–notably Robert Helpmann, Andrée Howard, John Cranko and Kenneth MacMillan.

Apart from the staging of new ballets, the great achievement of Ninette de Valois and her company in the fifties was the revival of two Diaghilev masterpieces which had been among the greatest successes of the Ballet-Russe companies in the thirties: these were 'The Firebird' and 'Petrushka', staged for the Sadler's Wells Ballet by Serge Grigoriev, who had been Diaghilev's régisseur-général, and his wife Lyubov Tchernicheva. These revivals were done with

the utmost care for detail, and were models of their kind: even such details as the exact weight of materials to be used in the costumes and the refinements in the lighting plot were reproduced, and once again Ninette de Valois put the world in her debt by saving masterpieces from oblivion.

Four different royal honours signposted the rising curve of achievement of Ninette de Valois and her company. The first was the award to her of the DBE in 1951–the equivalent of a knighthood–followed by the award of corresponding honours to Fonteyn (1959) and Ashton (1962). The fourth honour was the grant of a Royal Charter to the company in 1956: it now became known as the Royal Ballet, and its school as the Royal Ballet School.

In 1963 Dame Ninette retired as artistic director of the Royal Ballet, handing over this post to Ashton and concentrating on supervision of the Royal Ballet School. By this time the company she had founded and built up was world-famous and her ideas were influencing the development of national ballets all over the world.

Frederick Ashton

In 1935 Frederick Ashton became a permanent member of the Vic-Wells Ballet, and he soon became the company's chief choreographer. One gay divertissement-ballet, 'Les Patineurs', showed his talent at its best, and has been a feature of the repertoire ever since: his

fusion of neo-classical dance and skating movements was quite brilliant. But he also began to develop other aspects of his talent in ballets which he built around the fast-growing art of Margot Fonteyn: for her he choreographed a long series of romantic roles in neo-classical style, always using the same kind of patterns of classical steps which he evolved in the rehearsal room to suit her style, temperament and physique. The partnership between these two was extremely successful over a long period, and did much to help the company to build up its audience and its prestige.

When he began work on 'Symphonic Variations' in 1946 he started with a project for a large-scale semi-abstract ballet with a vaguely mythological theme. But, following a wise instinct, he changed his plans completely, cutting down the cast to six soloists and making the ballet completely abstract. Sophie Fedorovich, his Russian friend and mentor, provided him with an abstract décor suggesting a graph of mathematical equations, and simple elegant costumes derived from practice costume; soaking himself in the lyrical phrases of César Franck's music, Ashton clothed them in neo-classical enchainements very similar in many ways to those he had used in his pre-war ballets, but now he used them with a greater freshness and spontaneity.

In 1949, influenced by the rapidly growing interest the western world was taking in Soviet ballet, and the stress laid

in the Soviet Union on full-length ballets on the nineteenth-century Petipa model, Ashton staged *his* first full-length Petipa-style ballet: 'Cinderella', a new version of a ballet originally staged by Zakharov for the Bolshoi Ballet in 1945. 'Cinderella' was the first of many such reconstructions. In 1951 Ashton staged his own version of the one-act ballet 'Daphnis and Chloë', which Fokine had choreographed, to music by Ravel, without great success in 1911. Ashton's version had an effectively pathetic dance by Fonteyn, with bound hands, as a prisoner of the pirate chief, and some strong character dancing by Alexander Grant as the pirate chief. A year later Ashton staged another three-acter: 'Sylvia,' a reconstruction of a ballet originally produced in Paris in 1876. Then came 'Ondine', reconstructed from a ballet originally staged in London by Perrot in 1848. This time, instead of using the original music by Pugni, Ashton commissioned a score from the contemporary German composer Hans Werner Henze. There was little that was contemporary, however, about the Henze score: mostly he produced a pastiche of nineteenth-century music. The ballet had some strikingly romantic visual effects in which Ashton collaborated effectively with his designer, Lila de Nobile; in particular a scene in which Fonteyn, as Ondine, the Water-Sprite, appeared in a fountain, and a mysterious scene giving prominence to the corps de ballet danseuses wearing seductively décolleté Empire-line costumes. The most striking episode of all was a dance which had

also been the *clou* of the original production: Ondine's dance with her shadow.

In 1960 Ashton tackled a project which suited him perfectly: a new version of the eighteenth-century two-act comedy ballet 'La Fille Mal Gardée.' This ballet gave full scope to all of Ashton's talents, including his admirable sense of humour; and its success suggested that he really belonged in the eighteenth century rather than in the nineteenth.

'La Fille Mal Gardée' is by far the oldest important ballet to survive until the present day with a continuous choreographic tradition. The ballet was preserved in Russia (with changes and additions by various choreographers) right up to modern times, and was produced for various European companies by Alexandra Balashova, who danced the heroine Lise in Russia before the Revolution. It is an entrancing work, with many scenes which take one back to the beginning of the nineteenth century. Fortunately this traditional version has been preserved for posterity in a choreographic score made by the choreologist Monica Parker for the Institute of Choreology, with Balashova's collaboration.

Instead of commissioning a production of the traditional version, Ashton chose to choreograph a version which was quite new, except for one mime scene which he asked Karsavina to reproduce. His version inevitably lacks the magical period charm of the original, but it keeps faithfully to the story, and shows Ashton's talent for comedy at its

best—above all in the clog dance for Mother Simone, in which he cleverly combines authentic clog-dance steps with tap-dance patterns. This version has won for itself a permanent place in the Royal Ballet's repertoire.

In 1963 Ashton took over as director of the Royal Ballet. In a sense he was the obvious person to succeed Ninette de Valois, being far more experienced than anyone else in the company; but he would have been much happier not to take up the burden of administration, for it did not appeal to his temperament, and cut down the time he could spare for choreography. It was hardly surprising, therefore, that as soon as it was decently possible, in 1968, he announced his resignation—and arrangements were made to replace him in 1970 by the duumvirate of John Field and Kenneth MacMillan.

By far the most interesting of the works choreographed by Ashton after his appointment as director of the Royal Ballet was 'Monotones' (1965). In this ballet he returned to the abstraction of 'Symphonic Variations', but developed a new style inspired by the delicate plangent melody of Erik Satie's 'Gymnopédies'. He chose three dancers (Anthony Dowell, Robert Mead and Vyvyan Lorayne) who were distinguished by their musicality, sensitivity and pure classical line, dressed them all alike in white leotards and tights, and had them dance simple steps mainly in unison—thus giving the clearest expression of his ideal of romantic neo-classicism as something abstract and sexless. Later he added

Left Fokine's 'The Firebird' as revived by the Sadler's Wells Ballet in 1954; the final tableau, with Anya Linden as the Tsarevna and Michael Somes as Ivan Tsarevich.

Below Frederick Ashton's version of 'Cinderella', 1948, with Margot Fonteyn as Cinderella, David Blair as the Prince and Robert Helpmann and Frederick Ashton as the Ugly Sisters.

Left Fokine's 'The Firebird' as revived by the Sadler's Wells Ballet in 1954; the final tableau, with Anya Linden as the Tsarevna and Michael Somes as Ivan Tsarevich.

another pas de trois, but this was less magical.

Two ballets commissioned by Ashton were of the greatest artistic importance, opening up new possibilities to the company and in fact to world ballet. One was the revival of 'Les Noces', among the greatest of all the Diaghilev ballets. Nothing remotely like this masterly and quite revolutionary work had ever been staged by the Royal Ballet, and it says much for the spirit and talent of the dancers that they responded so well to the great demands made of them by Nijinska. At the end of the dress rehearsal she told the dancers that they performed it even better than the Diaghilev company for whom she created it. She had never thought to see this ballet performed again, she said, but now she could die happy.

Though 'Les Noces' preserved elements of the choreographic style of Nijinska's brother Nijinsky, as developed in the original version of 'The Rite of Spring', this ballet had been lost, and 'Les Noces' stood out clearly as unlike any other ballet: equal in every way to Stravinsky's magnificent choral music, yet taking its own line. The music is very complex, and Nijinska had seen that an equivalent complexity in the dancing would overwhelm the spectator; she therefore worked to achieve a noble, austere simplicity.

The dance-images, though inspired in their general style by Russian folk-dance steps, were in fact completely original, created for this ballet: there were only a small number of them, often performed by great blocks of dancers.

The other very important commission arranged by Ashton for the Royal Ballet was Tudor's 'Shadowplay' (1967): this brought back to Britain a great British choreographer who had been sadly missed, and released in him creative powers which had long been dammed up.

Above Bronislava Nijinska's 'Les Noces' as revived by the Royal Ballet in 1968, with Svetlana Beriosova as the Bride and Robert Mead as the Groom.

Top Frederick Ashton's version of 'Daphnis and Chloë', Sadler's Wells Ballet, 1951, with Christopher Gable as Daphnis performing the solo in which Daphnis competes with another shepherd.

Opposite Margot Fonteyn in Frederick Ashton's 'Symphonic Variations' with David Blair (Sadler's Wells Ballet, 1946).

*Below 'The Sleeping Beauty' with
Doreen Wells as Aurora (Royal Ballet,
Touring Section).*

*Right Revival of 'Petrushka' for the
Royal Ballet, with Alexander Grant as
Petrushka, Margot Fonteyn as the
Ballerina and Peter Clegg as the Moor.*

Above Kenneth MacMillan's version of 'Romeo and Juliet' with (l to r) Desmond Doyle as Tybalt, Rudolf Nureyev as Romeo and David Blair as Mercutio (Royal Ballet, 1955).

Opposite Robert Helpmann's 'Hamlet' as revived by the Royal Ballet, with Rudolf Nureyev as Hamlet and Lynn Seymour as Ophelia.

Other Choreographers

Andrée Howard was a founder-member of the Rambert company in 1930, and began to compose ballets for Marie Rambert in 1933, when she was only twenty-three. The best of these compositions were 'Death and the Maiden'— a translation into dance of the theme of the *andante cantabile* movement of a Schubert quartet—and 'Lady into Fox'. Another effective though rather long-winded work for Rambert was 'La Fête Etrange', inspired by an episode in the Alain-Fournier novel 'Les Grands Meaulnes', with nostalgic music by Fauré: this was designed for a small theatre, and a fairly small company, but with the help of the designer Sophie Federovich, Andrée Howard later made a successful large version for the Royal Ballet at Covent Garden.

She showed a very different side of her talent when she choreographed 'A Mirror for Witches' for the Sadler's Wells Ballet (1952).

Andrée Howard was always very sensitive to music, she was greatly helped in staging this dramatic ballet by the powerful dramatic music commissioned from Denis ApIvor. Though it was his first ballet score, ApIvor showed an astonishing grasp of the needs of choreography.

A year later Andrée Howard choreographed 'Veneziana', a light-hearted frolic with music by Donizetti arranged by ApIvor. Her life ended sadly with an overdose of sleeping tablets in 1968.

Australian-born Robert Helpmann joined the Vic-Wells Ballet in 1933, and showed such outstanding talent that a year later he became a leading dancer. In 'Hamlet', which he staged in 1942, he achieved a tour de force: a work which was really a mime-play rather than a ballet (having almost no dancing in it) but staged with great skill and theatrical sense, bringing together all the elements of theatre to make a powerful and unified impact. In violent contrast to all other English ballets of this period, 'Hamlet' had a serious and fascinating theme, worked out with real intelligence. Drawing on the theories of a number of Shakespearian critics, and above all by one who was much influenced by Freud, Helpmann presented the events of the Shakespeare play as hallucinations passing through Hamlet's mind as he was dying—the events being telescoped, distorted and fused together in a way which reflected Hamlet's inner conflicts.

John Cranko's great achievement is as a re-organiser of German ballet; but the basis for his career in Germany was established during his years with the Sadler's Wells Theatre Ballet and the Sadler's Wells Ballet. He was one of a number of South African dancers who left South Africa as soon as travel became possible after the War.

For some years he had only limited success with rather conventional romantic ballets. Then, in 1951, he found a subject, and music, which exactly suited his gifts: 'Pineapple Poll', a gay comedy based on one of W. S. Gilbert's 'Bab Ballads', with sparkling music taken from Gilbert and Sullivan operettas. This ballet became a favourite item in the repertoire of the Royal Ballet touring company.

In 1953 Kenneth MacMillan began his career as a choreographer, and in 1961 he staged a work which, for all its weaknesses, put him among the leading young choreographers in the world. This was 'The Invitation', staged for the touring company: here, for the first time, MacMillan found a subject which exactly suited his predilections, as well as a danseuse whose talents were such as to inspire him to create with a far greater intensity of feeling than ever before. He has done many fine things since 'The Invitation', but has never surpassed the finest scenes in this ballet.

Throughout his career MacMillan

24

has been obsessed by a figure of an innocent and vulnerable young girl, an outsider cut off from sympathy and love by ugliness, shyness, or some such disability, and overtaken by ill fortune. In 'The Invitation' MacMillan, taking advantage of the strong dramatic qualities of the young Canadian dancer Lynn Seymour, created an unforgettable figure: a very young girl, in love with a handsome boy, but cut off from him by awkward shyness. The climax of the ballet is the powerful garden scene; the innocent adolescent girl, torn apart by sexual feeling she cannot understand or cope with, comes to see an older man in a garden and behaves in a provocative manner; the encounter develops into a scene of rape. In contrast to every other scene MacMillan had staged up to then, this scene moved with extraordinary concentration and inevitability, without a single superfluous movement.

In 1965 MacMillan was given a very challenging assignment by the Royal Ballet: the full-length 'Romeo and Juliet'. This work, as created by Lavrovsky in Russia in 1940, had achieved great fame in the West through tours by Russian companies, and many different choreographers in the West had created their own versions. In its crowd scenes MacMillan's version could not compare with the original Lavrovsky version, for these were quite outside his range; but he came into his own in Act III, where for scene after scene all attention is concentrated on Juliet, and MacMillan found in the much-aggrieved and very young Juliet a figure well calculated to inspire him. In these scenes Juliet goes through a whole series of moods, ranging from passionate love for Romeo (in the bedroom scene) to leaden apathy in the scene with Paris, horror before taking the potion, and despair at waking up to find Romeo dead beside her in the tomb. Margot Fonteyn was not with the company when he staged the ballet, and he created the role of Juliet on Lynn Seymour; the result was that Margot Fonteyn was unhappy in it when she danced it at the première, and much less effective than Lynn Seymour, Antoinette Sibley or Merle Park. So MacMillan created a special version for Fonteyn, and this became one of her finest roles – as it was for the other three ballerinas.

In the summer of 1966 MacMillan was appointed director of the ballet company of the Deutsche Oper, one of Germany's leading ballet companies, and took Lynn Seymour with him. There he delighted in the challenge of having to create a considerable number of works each season. Moreover he had to take full responsibility for running the company: and this gave him experience which was invaluable to him when he became co-director of the Royal Ballet in 1970.

The new directors had the task of reorganizing the company, replacing the touring company with a relatively small and changing group of twenty-five soloists, and preparing a new repertoire for this group.

Margot Fonteyn

No-one who saw Margot Fonteyn dance Giselle on 19 January 1937 is likely to forget the experience. It was above all her dramatic intensity which made her stand out so strongly. From a purely technical point of view her dancing was good, but not all that good. But her gaiety and peasant simplicity in the earlier parts of the first act were very convincing; and when she began the mad scene she was overwhelming, with jagged, broken movements that completely expressed Giselle's agony of mind. From then on, for nearly twenty years, the achievements of the company were to a large extent based on the magnificent flowering of her talents. More aware than anyone of her technical weaknesses, she worked with many of the great Russian teachers of the day, learning something important from each, and perfecting a classical style of great beauty and fluidity that was capable of meeting the challenges of all the major classical roles. At the same time she widened her dramatic range: in her teens she was too full of girlish vitality to create mysterious, supernatural beings like Odette or the Giselle of Act II, but it was not long before she made these just as convincing as her other roles in the classics and in romantic roles created for her by Ashton. She showed, too, a superb sense of humour in 'Façade', but unfortunately became firmly type-cast as a romantic-classical ballerina.

At Covent Garden after the War she worked with Ashton on a series of roles of much the same kind as her earlier ones. There was Chloë in 'Daphnis and Chloë', in which she was specially moving in her pathetic dance with bound hands. And even more striking was her interpretation of the water-sprite Ondine, in which she used her hands with poetry and subtlety to suggest the watery nature of the role.

In 1954, with the revival of 'The Firebird' to celebrate the twenty-fifth

anniversary of the death of Diaghilev, Fonteyn found herself faced with a new and very difficult challenge. In the role of the Firebird, Fokine (taking much from the East) had created something really fresh; it was far outside Fonteyn's previous experience; but helped by Karsavina, the original Firebird, she triumphed.

In the sixties two things brought about a major change in her career. One was her decision, after two decades of being the company's star, to leave its permanent staff, returning for various periods during the year as a guest artist, but doing what she liked for the rest of the year. The other great change arose from the appearance on the Western ballet scene of Rudolf Nureyev and his association with her at Covent Garden and elsewhere. Working alongside Nureyev, Fonteyn was inspired to dance with a delightful new freshness and feeling.

Other Leading Dancers

The Royal Ballet has a remarkable variety of highly talented and individual danseuses. When Margot Fonteyn left the company Svetlana Beriosova became prima ballerina: tall, beautiful, with long legs and a broad, serene flow of movement in pure Russian style, she is the embodiment of the classical-romantic ballerina; but when occasion offers she can show outstanding ability in dramatic and comic roles which break away from this romantic image. Merle Park is supremely musical, intelligent, versatile and creative, transforming each existing role into something wonderfully fresh, and adding her own magic to roles created for her. Antoinette Sibley has a

perfect physique and wonderfully polished line, as well as very expressive arms
and dramatic power. Doreen Wells
stands out because of her easy and natural
style, clean line and extraordinary charm.
Monica Mason is splendid in character
and dramatic roles which give scope to
her powerful attack. Deirdre O'Conaire
has versatility, dramatic intensity, a pure
classical Russian style with splendid
breadth of movement and a very Irish
sense of humour. Ann Jenner and Jen-
nifer Penner are astonishingly alike in
some ways–they both have great precision of movement–but differ a good
deal in personality.

The company is by no means so rich
in male talent, but it has a few remarkable artists. Anthony Dowell has a rare
grace and fluidity, a strong technique,
wonderful line (with a high supple ex-
tension) and a curiously aloof stage
presence: if only he had temperament
and dramatic ability as well, he would
astonish the world. David Wall has a fine
presence, good line and an attractive
personality, and has successfully tackled
an amazing variety of roles.

Left above David Wall in the leading
male role of Frederick Ashton's
'Sinfonietta', performed by the Royal
Ballet Touring Section.

Left below Svetlana Beriosova in 1953,
rehearsing the title role of Frederick
Ashton's version of 'Sylvia' with Philip
Chatfield as Aminta.

This page Deirdre O'Conaire rehearsing
the role of Grisi in Anton Dolin's version
of 'Le Pas de Quatre', staged for the
opening gala of the Adeline Senée Theatre
with dancers of the Royal Ballet.

The Royal Ballet School

In the thirties, when the Vic-Wells Ballet performed at the Sadler's Wells Theatre, the Vic-Wells School was carried on in a big room in the theatre. After the War, the school was re-established, on a greatly expanded basis, in two different buildings. The junior school, a boarding school at which classes were given in ordinary school subjects as well as in dancing, was established at White Lodge, a former royal residence in the middle of Richmond Park on the outskirts of London, while the senior school, where the whole stress was on ballet classes, was in a rather more accessible district near Hammersmith.

Since the senior school offers a chance, even if only a small one, of joining one of the world's greatest ballet companies, it attracts the best students from a great many British schools; and fine students from other schools all over the world. In a vintage year, the quality of the dancing at the annual school matinée at Covent Garden is so high that it is quite impossible to believe that the young dancers are not experienced professionals.

BALLET RAMBERT

Above Ninette de Valois taking a class with students of the Royal Ballet Senior School.

Opposite Marie Rambert with Lucette Aldous, in the wings during a performance in which Lucette Aldous danced the title role in 'La Sylphide' (Ballet Rambert).

Next page Norman Morrice's '1-2-3' with Christopher Bruce and Mary Willis (reorganized Ballet Rambert).

Born in Warsaw, and trained in Dalcroze Eurythmics, Marie Rambert was flung in at the deep end when Diaghilev asked her to help Nijinsky with the musical aspects of 'The Rite of Spring', which has one of the most rhythmically complex of all scores. Being very musical and highly intelligent, she did a first-rate job, helping Nijinsky to come to grips with every note of the music. This production was crucial in the development of both ballet and modern dance, and made a deep impression on Marie Rambert; when she established her company in London in 1930 (and thus started the renaissance in British ballet) she ran it in such a way as to foster creativity above all. Even though the dancers appearing each Sunday at the Mercury Theatre were not paid, they showed remarkable professionalism and maturity, and there was a notable flowering of choreography: she gave opportunities to a number of talented people including Ashton, who eventually moved on to the Wells, Andrée Howard, and Antony Tudor. Though he eventually set up his own company, Tudor created masterpieces for Rambert which made her company unique in the world, and they remained at the heart of its repertoire.

The company ceased to exist for a time during the War, but was reformed by the government organisation CEMA, with Marie Rambert as artistic director. It enjoyed renewed success and reached its peak in 1944, when it contained a number of outstanding dancers, and had a magnificent repertoire of ballets by Tudor, Ashton, de Valois, Andrée Howard and others. But Marie Rambert failed to provide the company with a London home after the War, and so the company lost most of its good dancers as well as its creative impetus. It now spent the year touring the provinces, performing mainly ballets like 'Coppélia' which theatre managers considered best suited to the taste of their audiences. There were short annual seasons at Sadler's Wells, during which some major ballets were performed, above all the Tudor masterpieces: but these were under-rehearsed, and degenerated through be-

ing passed from dancer to dancer without
attention from the choreographer. New
ballets were few and disappointing. By
far the best item in the repertoire was an
admirable production of 'Giselle', originally staged for the company by the very
young Joyce Graeme in 1945-6. This had
simplicity, style and a fine period feeling:
all it lacked was a great classical ballerina
to do justice to the title role.

In 1960 Marie Rambert commissioned a splendid production of the
Bournonville ballet 'La Sylphide' from
the Danish dancer Elsa Marianne von
Rosen. This had a very polished performance in the title role from the young
Australian ballerina Lucette Aldous,
whose acting abilities were still unde-
veloped but who was technically outstanding. It also had a superb performance from the wonderfully versatile and
imaginative Gillian Martlew, hiding
her beauty behind a grotesque make-up
as Madge the Witch. Two years later
Marie Rambert commissioned a revival
of Gorsky's version of 'Don Quixote'.
This was a spectacular bravura work, ill-

suited to the small Rambert company,
but Aldous gave a jewel-like perfection
and great vitality to the leading role of
Kitry, while Anna Truscott was magnificent in two other roles.

In fact things seemed to be going well,
and for a time even the Tudor ballets had
some superb London performances in
certain roles by Gillian Martlew and
Anna Truscott. But the company became more and more out of touch with
artistic and financial reality, falling between several stools. With costs going
up, and receipts falling, it could now
afford to stage only one new ballet a year
(by Norman Morrice, its associate director); and both Gillian Martlew and
Anna Truscott gave up their dancing
careers in despair.

Norman Morrice saw that there was no
future for a relatively small company
trying, with only limited success, to do
things which three larger companies,
the two Royal Ballet companies and the
Festival Ballet, were already doing. He
proposed a complete reorganization, returning the company to its pre-war

creative role. The new company, following the example set by Tudor's company of 1938-40 and Nederlands Dans Theater, would be a small one, consisting only of soloists; like NDT and various American companies it would bring together ballet and modern dance; it would commission new works by a wide variety of choreographers and it would retain the Tudor ballets as its modern classics at the heart of the repertoire.

Norman Morrice's proposal won the approval of the Arts Council, which provided the necessary capital grant and subsidy, and the reorganized company (some of the dancers from the old company joined by a number of promising young dancers) made its début at the small Jeannetta Cochrane Theatre in November, 1966. The début was disappointing, but within a few months Morrice began to commission works of outstanding value, the company developed very fast, and his ideals soon began to be realized.

By this time some of the best dancers and choreographers in the United States were combining the techniques and traditions of ballet and modern dance with assurance and fluency. Among them was Glen Tetley. The first ballet he staged for the Ballet Rambert was 'Pierrot Lunaire'; this was in fact his first major work, originally staged by him in New York in 1963 (when he himself danced Pierrot), and later revived for Nederlands Dans Theater. Both musically and thematically this ballet – based on an early Schönberg suite of songs using a strange cross between speaking and singing – was a great challenge to the choreographer; but the theme clearly appealed to him strongly, and he established the characters of Pierrot, Brighella and Columbine, as well as the many changes of mood, with great clarity. Working with the Rambert dancers, he cast the ballet perfectly, and worked with skill and sympathy to get fine performances from all three of his chosen artists – Christopher Bruce, Sandra Craig and Jonathan Taylor. In fact the performance given by the young and inexperienced Christopher Bruce was remarkable for its maturity, depth and sensitivity, and showed him to be one of the most sensitive and creative male dancers in the world.

A few months later Morrice commissioned another work which contributed an incalculable amount to the artistic maturity of the whole company: Anna Sokolow's 'Deserts'. Anna Sokolow is an American modern-dance choreographer who began as one of Graham's first dancers, but broke away and established herself as a choreographer with a tough, bitter style of her own, depicting with tremendous intensity the loneliness, frustration and violence of life in the big city. Much of her work is performed to jazz music; in 'Deserts', however, she

used music by Varèse which was partly electronic, and achieved her effects in a much more abstract way than usual, using complex group patterns rather than solo dancing. She worked on the dancers with her habitual passionate intensity, and they matured in an extraordinary way under the impact of her personality and her demands.

Another major success was the revival of 'L'Après-Midi d'un Faune'. When Nijinsky created this ballet in 1912, he broke away from existing traditions to an amazing extent, creating dance-images of a new type; and it might almost be considered the first major work of modern dance. But the choreography, being so unusual, might easily have been lost after the death of Diaghilev: fortunately Marie Rambert had commissioned a production of it in 1931 from Woizikowsky (a leading Diaghilev dancer), with William Chappell in the title role, and had had the foresight to take a film of the production. With the aid of this film it proved possible to revive the masterpiece with astonishing fidelity of detail and atmosphere; and, what was no less important, the company now had a male dancer able to dance Nijinsky's role with the right sort of sensitivity and magic–Christopher Bruce.

Taking advantage of the fast-developing talents of the Rambert dancers, Glen Tetley created with them a major new work in November, 1967: 'Ziggurat'. For music he used some very strange electronic music by Stockhausen, making it a basis for the development of a very complex theme. There was a line of men in cobwebby tights, moving across the stage in a series of great lunging leaps that suggested that they had been birds in a previous incarnation; Tetley, taking up an idea already used by various contemporary composers, encouraged each dancer to create his own detailed patterns within the general pattern of movement. The finest episode in a complex and fascinating ballet was a mysterious pas de deux, performed by Bob Smith and Sandra Craig over a sheet of PVC in a diagonal shaft of light. The ballet used very complex projections (by Alan Cunliffe) and a visually exciting décor of tubular steel that moved as part of the choreography; the design, in fact, of all the new ballets staged by the new Ballet Rambert was fresh, imaginative and effective.

Morrice's own development as a choreographer was now progressing well, partly because of the exciting atmosphere of the reorganized company and partly because of the stimulus he had received while working for the outstanding Israeli modern-dance company Batsheva. In Tel Aviv, faced with a company of modern dancers which included a group of male dancers with exciting toughness, attack and virility,

as well as some highly talented New-York-trained female soloists, Morrice created a work of delightful wit and inventiveness. This was 'Rehearsal . . . ! ?', which showed a choreographer working on the final stages of the creation of a ballet; later, in 1968, he created another effective work, '1–2–3', and added this to the Rambert repertoire. In contrast to the ballets he had been creating for the Rambert in recent years, '1–2–3' had a simple theme, with only three characters –two young boys and a girl; Morrice really got inside this theme, being clearly influenced by Graham and Tetley but developing his own ideas in his own way.

Another important new development was the organization by Morrice of workshop performances in which young choreographers, in collaboration with young designers of the Central School of Arts and Crafts, were given the chance to stage ballets with the company. The new company still had certain weaknesses: its programmes were generally too much in the same tense and desperate mood, the Tudor classics suffered from decades of having been transmitted between dancers without the intervention of the choreographer, and there was too much concentration on modern-dance technique at the expense of ballet technique; but these were of small importance compared with its great achievements and rapid progress.

In 1969 Christopher Bruce, with his second ballet 'Living Space', showed himself as a choreographer of exceptional originality and promise. Here he succeeded with remarkable skill in solving the difficult problem of setting choreography to the words of a poem.

Left above 'Giselle' *as performed by the
Ballet Rambert c. 1960, with Alida Belair
as Giselle and Kenneth Bannerman as
Albrecht (Ballet Rambert).*

*Left below Norman Morrice soon after his
reorganization of the Ballet Rambert, in
the wings of the Jeanetta Cochrane
Theatre.*

*Below David Lichine's version of 'The
Nutcracker' for the Festival Ballet.*

ANTONY TUDOR

Antony Tudor joined Marie Rambert's company at its formation in 1930, and was soon playing a role of crucial importance in the renaissance of British ballet, helping it to strike out on its own path.

In his sixth ballet ('Atalanta of the East', 1933) he found his way into a new creative world through an unsuccessful – but artistically very significant – attempt at a ballet in Indian style, inspired by the visit of Uday Shankar's company of Indian dancers: in this work he learned how to use arms and hands in a new way, and began to develop a very fluid, original and expressive way of setting movements to music. His next ballet – 'The Planets' – showed him successfully applying what he had discovered, and also taking ideas from the German modern-dance work by Kurt Jooss, 'The Green Table'.

Tudor's first major work was 'Lilac Garden' – a masterpiece which has been performed by companies all over the world, though it demands a subtlety of interpretation which very few dancers can provide. By this time (1936) Tudor had developed ways of expressing nuances of feeling, mood and character which were new to ballet, expanding the scope of the art rather as Proust did with the novel and Chekhov with the drama. Tudor showed four people of Edwardian times at a crisis in their lives: a bride facing a marriage of convenience to a man she does not love, her lover, the future husband, and the mistress he is abandoning. The characters and the changing moods of the two women were shown with poetic dance-images of the greatest subtlety.

Like the greatest works of Fokine and Nijinsky, 'Dark Elegies' (1937) transformed the art of ballet, creating a new language of expressive imagery in which every dance-image was newly minted for the occasion. It is possible to trace in this ballet the influence of ideas from German and American modern dance, folk-dances, classical Indian dancing, Kabuki and even tap-dancing: but fused together with such assurance and imagination that the patterns seemed all of a piece, belonging to this ballet and no other. The ballet, based on Mahler's great song cycle 'Kindertotenlieder', was concerned with parents in a fishing village mourning the death of their children; the theme was treated in an abstract way, and the dancers moved with impassive features, as if taking part in a ritual; yet the projection of feeling was extremely powerful.

'Dark Elegies' needed space to move in, being quite unsuited to the Mercury stage, and in fact soon after producing it Tudor left the Ballet Club to form his own company, the London Ballet performing at Toynbee Hall in the East End. This company established a pattern which was to become typical of creative ballet companies many years later: it had no corps de ballet, only soloists (or potential soloists), and a repertoire consisting entirely of new ballets designed for such a group; the dancers received wages, though small ones. For this company Tudor revived the bitterly satirical ballet 'The Judgment of Paris', in which the myth was given an Edwardian twist by showing an old roué visiting a brothel; the three girls performed wonderfully bad dances, using great skill to show complete lack of skill.

But this was before the days of government subsidies and the company fell into debt, due in part to the remoteness of the theatre, so in 1939 Tudor joined the newly formed and well-endowed American company Ballet Theater. In due course he became its chief choreographer and artistic administrator; in this way he became for a time the dominant influence on American ballet. His most perfect work for Ballet Theater was 'Pillar of Fire', based on Schönberg's 'Verklärte Nacht'. This told the story of the unhappy, frustrated Hagar and her two sisters, and showed her progress through a variety of experiences to self-knowledge and fulfilment. The style was much more classical than that of 'Dark Elegies', though still very different from that of any previous ballet. In the two dramatic pas de deux, Tudor brought a new intensity and concentration of expressiveness into the portrayal of emotional interactions between a man and a woman. The leading roles were taken by the great American dancer Nora Kaye, who matured rapidly under Tudor's guidance, by Hugh Laing, who had been Tudor's principal male dancer in London, and by Tudor himself.

In 1944 Tudor created for Ballet Theater 'Undertow', which was built round the central role of The Transgressor – a role of Hamlet-like complexity, making greater demands on the interpreter than any previous male role, and danced with great power by Hugh Laing.

During the fifties and early sixties Tudor devoted himself mainly to teaching in New York at the Metropolitan Opera Ballet School and the Juilliard School of Music; most of the leading American classical and modern dancers came to his classes, which showed a fresh and creative approach to the classical technique. Since his students included some major American choreographers of the future (Alvin Ailey, Paul Taylor, Glen Tetley and many others) they had great influence, in conjunction with his

Above Antony Tudor's revival of his ballet 'Lilac Garden' for the Royal Ballet in 1969, with Antoinette Sibley as Caroline and Anthony Dowell as Her Lover.

Opposite above Antony Tudor rehearsing his 'Shadowplay' with Merle Park as the Celestial and Anthony Dowell as the Boy with Matted Hair (Royal Ballet).

Opposite below Antony Tudor's 'Judgment of Paris' with (l to r) Valerie Marsh as Minerva, Elsa Recagno as Juno and Gillian Martlew as Venus.

ballets; 'Dark Elegies', in particular, had even more influence on American modern dance than on American ballet.

Though he lived in the United States, Tudor remained very English, and it is likely that his exile from England had a depressing effect on his creative impulses. In 1966 a fortunate accident gave him the opportunity to do something he had longed to do ever since the days when he danced in the Vic-Wells Ballet, but was given no opportunity to create works for it: Kenneth MacMillan left unexpectedly to take up an appointment as director of the ballet company of the Deutsche Oper in Berlin, and to fill the gap caused by his absence Ashton commissioned Tudor to create a new work for the Royal Ballet. Tudor felt very nervous about this commission, for it meant a great deal to him, and he made many experiments with the dancers before he settled on the form of his new work, 'Shadowplay'. Finally he found his true path, and the result was a strange and fascinating work, very Oriental in texture, and quite unlike anything ever performed by the company (or, indeed, anything Tudor himself had done). The story and its treatment showed the result of the years in which Tudor had immersed himself in Buddhism, yoga and in fact all aspects of Oriental culture: using music by the French composer Koechlin (itself based on Kipling's story 'The Jungle Book') it showed a boy setting out into the world in search of

knowledge and wisdom, meeting monkeys (symbolizing the chaos and vulgarity of everyday life), and facing the dangers of corruption from a mysterious Terrestrial and a strange love-goddess (the Celestial). One might have expected to see the boy portrayed by a strong dramatic dancer, of the Hugh Laing type: instead, Tudor gave the part to Anthony Dowell, and had him move through it in a serene, impassive and elegant manner which was very Japanese, with great emphasis on purity of classical line. But Tudor treated the role of the Celestial very differently: he gave this role to Merle Park, taking full advantage of her intelligence, musicality, intuition and imagination to create with her help an image of a seductive but very dangerous Indian goddess.

With this ballet Tudor found his way back to creative work at the highest level: it was a turning point in his life and in the development of British ballet. In fact, it was not long before Ashton commissioned from Tudor a production of 'Lilac Garden' for the main company, and a new ballet for the touring company.

The first night of 'Lilac Garden' at Covent Garden in 1968 was a near-disaster, because of miscasting of all the leading roles. But when the second cast took over, the effect was as overwhelming as that of an Old Master, cleaned of layer upon layer of dark varnish. As the romantic Caroline, forced to marry a man she does not love, Antoinette Sibley

gave the performance of her life: like Tudor, she had been deeply influenced by Indian dancing at an early and crucial phase of her career, and now she used her arms with the greatest subtlety and expressiveness in gestures which Tudor produced to show even more than their original freshness and poignancy. Much the same thing happened to the role of Caroline's sister; originally this had been a minor role, but now Tudor assigned it to Deirdre O'Conaire and achieved from her a performance of such delicacy and depth that the ballet as a whole achieved a new and more satisfying balance between its various moods and conflicts.

Tudor's new ballet for the touring company, 'Knight Errant', was in a style quite different from that of 'Shadowplay', and suggested that he was now developing in a variety of new directions. He based this ballet on a letter in the greatest French novel of the eighteenth century, 'Les Liaisons Dangereuses', using a neo-classical style in a witty satirical way, with formal patterns overlaying depths of ruthless cynicism; his choreography made admirable use of the charm, elegance and dramatic power of David Wall in the leading role, and drew from young Margaret Barbieri a performance of astonishing maturity and sophistication as a seduced wife: she was simultaneously demure and randy, innocent and depraved, in a way that only Tudor could achieve with an artist of rare talent.

FESTIVAL BALLET

In contrast to other British companies, the Festival Ballet, founded by Anton Dolin and Dr Julian Braunsweg in 1950, has always been very cosmopolitan, drawing its principals from many countries and often employing guest artists. In its artistic policy it has continued on much the same lines as the similarly cosmopolitan Ballet-Russe companies which came into existence after the death of Diaghilev, and were an important feature of the international ballet scene throughout the thirties, forties and fifties. The Festival repertoire was built around the familiar nineteenth-century 'classics', with the addition of the most popular Diaghilev ballets ('Petrushka', 'Prince Igor' and 'Schéhérazade'). Revivals were also commissioned from two living Russian choreographers (Massine and Lichine), the most successful of these being the light-entertainment ballet 'Graduation Ball', choreographed by Lichine with admirable décor in nineteenth-century style by the great old designer Alexandre Benois, who had been one of the main architects of the Russian renaissance in ballet, and worked with Diaghilev. Another successful revival was Dolin's 'Le Pas de Quatre', based on a ballet which Perrot had staged in London in 1843 as a showpiece for four of the greatest ballerinas of the day and created by Dolin for Ballet Theater in 1940. Dolin took on some remarkable male dancers, notably John Gilpin, Oleg Briansky and the character

dancer Vassili Trunoff (quite splendid in 'Prince Igor'); in fact the high standard of the male dancing has remained a distinctive feature of the Festival Ballet ever since.

The company suffered the first of many severe blows in 1952 when Markova left; but Dolin found a replacement in Belinda Wright, a young and highly talented dancer, though very different from Markova in style and temperament.

Having neither a subsidy nor, since the tearing down of the Stoll Theatre, a regular London home, the company seemed unlikely to survive for long, since it depended on presenting ballet as a money-making, as distinct from a money-using, proposition. This had been possible for Ballet-Russe companies before the War, but since then all costs had increased enormously – far more than seat prices. Fortunately for the company, Dr Braunsweg was very enterprising, and in 1952 the company achieved a solid basis in London. Every summer it came to the newly built Royal Festival Hall, by arrangement with the London County Council (which owned and managed the hall), and it also gave Christmas seasons there in which it performed only 'The Nutcracker'. The rest of the year it toured very widely, both in Britain and on the Continent.

During the next few years the company had its ups and downs, and even

Opposite Jack Carter's 'Witch Boy', with John Gilpin in the title role, and Anita Landa as Barbara Allen (Festival Ballet).

Top Vladimir Bourmeister's 'The Snow Maiden' with Irina Borowska in the title role (Festival Ballet, 1961).

Above Harald Lander's 'Etudes', with John Gilpin (Festival Ballet).

went into liquidation at one point. But
Dr Braunsweg had remarkable resili-
ence, and somehow kept the company
going. The repertoire was strengthened
in 1955 by the addition of 'Etudes',
which the Danish choreographer Harald
Lander had originally created in 1948 for
the Royal Danish Ballet. Toni Lander, a
fine Danish ballerina who was then part
of the company, was outstanding in the
principle role, and the company's leading male dancer John Gilpin was no less
so in the principal male role.

In 1957 the repertoire received the
further reinforcement of 'The Witch
Boy', a strong dramatic ballet which
Jack Carter had staged the year before
for the Ballet der Lage Lande in Holland.
Before staging 'The Witch Boy' Carter
had already had a good deal of experience of choreography; but in this ballet
he found a subject–an adaptation of the
sinister legend of Barbara Allen–which
suited him perfectly, and he composed a
ballet of such dramatic intensity and
clarity of detail (not a step was wasted)
that it has never lost its appeal. One of
Carter's great merits is that he is a fine
producer, able to get the best out of all
his artists, and he did wonders with the

Festival dancers when he directed them
in 'The Witch Boy'.

Dolin remained as artistic director
until 1961, when he left, and John Gilpin
took over. The next few years saw the
production of a series of large-scale, full-
length ballets: 'The Snow Maiden',
staged by the Soviet choreographer
Vladimir Bourmeister, and 'Peer Gynt'
and 'Swan Lake', staged by another
Russian, Vaslav Orlikovsky. It was in
'Swan Lake' (1964), performed at the
big New Victoria cinema in London,
that Lucette Aldous had a triumphant
success as Odette-Odile: by now she had
matured artistically, and showed a remarkable capacity for getting inside the
role.

In 1965 the theatrical impresario
Donald Albery took over the company
as administrator, Norman MacDowell
became artist director, and Jack Carter
became resident choreographer. Carter
was now commissioned to stage a series
of large-scale productions of nineteenth-
century ballets, and two of these (new
versions of productions he had already
staged in Buenos Aires) were of exceptional importance. For 'Swan Lake' he
reconstructed as far as possible the

original Moscow production, adding
choreography to music unused in the
familiar St Petersburg production, and
allotting the role of Odette-Odile to
two different ballerinas. The reconstruction was done with taste and intelligence,
and Carter drew admirable performances from Maryon Lane (Odette),
Lucette Aldous (Odile) and John Gilpin
(Siegfried). The last act alone was a little
weak: otherwise the new version stood
up very well.

No less impressive was Carter's production of 'The Sleeping Beauty' in
1968, by which time the ballerina Beryl
Grey had taken over as artistic director,
with Wilfrid Stiff as administrator. This
production had some remarkable Auro-
ras–notably the Russian ballerina Galina
Samtsova, from Kiev, who had developed remarkably while in the company, showing a noble Russian breadth
of movement; and Lucette Aldous, now
a guest artist on leave from the Royal
Ballet, gave the role a fine-spun delicacy
and richness of detail. By this time the
company was receiving a subsidy from
the Arts Council, and financially it was·
more solidly established than ever before.

North America

BALLET

*Previous page Alwin Nikolais' 'Imago';
the Mantis scene, in which the dancers
form abstract patterns derived in part from
those of the Praying Mantis.*

*Above George Balanchine watching a
rehearsal of the New York City Ballet.*

*Opposite George Balanchine's 'Apollo'
with Suzanne Farrell as Terpsichore and
Jacques d'Amboise as Apollo
(New York City Ballet, 1957).*

George Balanchine and the New York City Ballet

The American ballet world contrasts in the most striking way with the American modern dance world. From the late twenties onwards, American modern dance has thrown up an astonishing variety of styles, personalities, techniques and aesthetic outlooks, and there has always been an open door to new ideas and new creative talent. The opposite is true of American ballet: ever since about 1950 this has been largely dominated by the ideas and the aesthetic outlook of one man, George Balanchine. He owes a great deal to his early years in the Maryinsky Theatre in St Petersburg/ Petrograd and has been powerfully influenced by the Petipa ballets which dominated the Maryinsky repertoire in his youth: in fact much of his choreography represents a reworking of enchainements from little-known Petipa ballets. The other major influence on Balanchine in his youth was the experimental productions of Goleizovsky and others in a hectic period in Petrograd after the Revolution; to this was added the very powerful impact of the gimmicky, vogue-chasing atmosphere of the Diaghilev Ballet in its final years.

His highly individual attitude to the classical tradition is to be seen most clearly in his approach to eighteenth- and nineteenth-century music. In what he calls his 'classic ballets' he commonly treats this in a way which is strange to the point of freakishness; like Petipa dealing with music by Minkus or Drigo, he works out the patterns he likes, and sets them to the music in a rather arbitrary way; he uses a great deal of repetition and symmetry, and seems to revel in the clichés of nineteenth-century ballet with a nostalgia which is oddly at variance with his avant-garde beginnings and with other aspects of his creative activities.

Though most of the ballets which Balanchine created for Diaghilev were merely freakish, he did create two which proved to have a lasting quality. 'Apollon Musagète' had a slight thread of mythological story, but this story was not treated very seriously: essentially this was an abstract ballet, and the first of a long line of abstract works. As for 'The Prodigal Son' (1929), this showed a very strange mixture of gimmickry and serious dramatic intent: there were many childish stunts, such as having a girl passed over the heads of the line of men, but the story was told with a sure sense of theatre, and admirable consistency of style.

Four years after the death of Diaghilev Balanchine was fortunate enough to find a patron in Lincoln Kirstein, a member of a wealthy American merchant family. Kirstein brought Balanchine to America in 1935 to establish the School of American Ballet as well as the first of a number of American companies, and they have worked closely together ever since. But Balanchine's great influence in the United States dates from 1949, when he and Kirstein received an invitation as significant as that received by Ninette de Valois from Lilian Baylis eighteen years previously. Morton Baum, chairman of the finance committee of the New York City Center (run by the City of New York) invited Balanchine and Kirstein to move their company (Ballet Society) into the City Center, alongside the existing opera and ballet companies. This created a revolutionary change in the status and prospects of the Balanchine-Kirstein company: it now found itself in the same very favourable position as the Vic-Wells Ballet had done in the thirties, with a permanent home in the country's greatest city, and helped financially by being part of a much larger organization. As in London, these advantages were overwhelming: the New York City Ballet soon pulled ahead of Ballet

Theater, taking over its finest dancers, notably the great Tudor dancer Nora Kaye, Hugh Laing and Diana Adams, and the very talented young dancer and choreographer Jerome Robbins.

It already possessed the remarkable artist Maria Tallchief, of Amerindian descent, who had studied with Nijinska before coming to the School of American Ballet; Balanchine made her his prima ballerina and then his wife, a pattern characteristic of his whole career. With his penchant for youth, he liked taking promising young dancers and helping them to develop artistically; but as they matured into great artists he invariably lost interest, and transferred his interest to another promising young dancer.

There was a typical example of such a change-over in the early years of the NYCB, when Tanaquil LeClercq became the favoured dancer, later also the wife, and flowered rapidly under Balanchine's tutelage. This remarkable artist stood out by her elegance, versatility, creativity, charm, vivacity and wit; and in 'Bourrée Fantasque' (1949) Balanchine gave her an admirable chance to show all these qualities by creating for her a comedy role–that of an elegant ballerina paired with a well-meaning but inept partner (Jerome Robbins)–in which he encouraged her to create much of the detail for herself which she did with enormous success. Tragically, this delectable artist caught polio in 1956 and became partially paralysed.

Working under what were for him almost ideal conditions, Balanchine created at a great rate: he was concerned above all with the present and future and very little with the past, taking the view that ballets are essentially ephemeral ('like butterflies', as he said) and that what mattered was to go on creating new things in tune with his feelings of the moment; even when he revived ballets from the past, such as 'The Firebird',

'Swan Lake Act II' and 'The Nut-cracker', he produced them with his new choreography.

Many of his new ballets were 'classic ballets', performed without décor by danseuses in Petipa-type tutus, with male dancers used mainly as supports for the girls, as in the days of Petipa; and these ballets tended to dominate the programmes. But in 1957 he began to break through into a new world with 'Agon', choreographed to a fascinating score in which Stravinsky, influenced in his old age by the long-dead Webern, began to move towards serialism, even though his approach was still neo-classi-cal, in the sense that he modelled the music on dances in a French dance manual of the seventeenth century. Balanchine set himself the enterprising task of finding an equivalent in move-ment of Stravinsky's progress towards serialism. Here Balanchine's outstanding cleverness and musicality (often mis-applied in the past) were put to admirable use. As was often the case in Balanchine's work, the climax of the ballet was the big pas de deux: here Stravinsky moved a long way towards Webern, using phrases and rhythms quite different from those of the earlier sections; Balanchine did not quite meet this challenge, but he created some striking and original pat-terns with bold distortions of classroom steps.

After tackling Webernesque music at the end of 'Agon', Balanchine moved on to Webern himself in 'Episodes' – a work which he staged in collaboration with Martha Graham. The first part, danced by Graham and her company, told the story of Mary Tudor, with the dancers in stiff, elaborate Elizabethan costumes; in the second part the Balanchine com-pany (with Paul Taylor), wearing stark black-and white practice dress, perfor-med abstract evolutions in which Balan-chine, contrary to his habit when using nineteenth-century music, showed the

Above Maria Tallchief rehearsing a Balanchine role.

Opposite Jerome Robbins' 'Afternoon of a Faun' with Wilma Curley and John Jones (Ballets: USA).

utmost respect for what Webern was saying. This style was a development out of that of the pas de deux in 'Agon', but the stage patterns were far more complex.

Just at this time two remarkable young dancers were coming to the fore. Mimi Paul trained originally at the Washington School of the Ballet: with her elegant long legs, superb sense of line, mysterious personality and powerful stage presence she generated her own kind of magic in a variety of roles. In fact she had many of the same qualities as previous Balanchine prima ballerinas, as well as some that were unique to her. But she was not what Balanchine wanted at this stage in his development, and in 1968 she left him, leaving a great gap. In fact it was Suzanne Farrell whom Balanchine chose to make his leading dancer. She had exactly the qualities he wanted at this stage in his career–a cool, aloof, almost neutral clarity of movement, performing the patterns of movement exactly as laid down by him, without adding any magic or poetry of her own. So Suzanne Farrell became the star of the company, dancing all the important roles, until she married in 1969 and left the company. By the beginning of 1970 it looked as if the delightful artist Kay Mazzo, up to then distinguished for her performances in ballets by Jerome Robbins, would become the female star of the NYCB.

On the whole, over the years, Balanchine's solo male dancers were far less impressive than his ballerinas. One exception was the splendid Negro Arthur Mitchell; and another was Edward Villela, who trained at the School of American Ballet, and joined the company in 1957. Villela showed all the virtues proper to a great danseur noble–grace, high elevation, a powerful technique, and so on; and when he took over the title role in 'The Prodigal Son' in 1960 he had a rare chance to show that he

also possessed dramatic ability. By then he was clearly one of the world's greatest dancers, something very important to a company where the main emphasis had been on the dancing of the girls.

In 1964 the New York City Ballet moved from its old home at the New York City Center (which was ill-suited to ballet) to the New York State Theater at Lincoln Center, alongside a new theatre for the Metropolitan Opera, a new concert hall, a new drama theatre and a new building housing the Juilliard School of Music. The New York State Theater was built at a cost of nineteen million dollars, being designed by the architect with Balanchine's requirements in mind. The NYCB became the resident company at this theatre, performing there on its own for about twenty weeks in the year, and thus achieving a performing status unique in the world: a status in fact corresponding to the real nature and needs of ballet.

Jerome Robbins

No choreographer has had a more varied career than Jerome Robbins. He had training in modern dance, ballet, Spanish and Oriental dance and drama; he danced in every sort of ballet company; he created many different kinds of choreography, not only for dance companies but also for stage and film musicals: his musical 'West Side Story' was a masterpiece of total theatre, bringing together acting, singing and dancing in a compelling synthesis.

Between 1949 and 1963 he was associate artistic director of the New York City Ballet; and during this period he also formed and ran his own superb company, Ballets: USA, producing some delightful ballets in the eclectic jazz-dance style of which he is a master. The repertoire of this company also included the wittily satirical 'Afternoon of a Faun', created by Robbins for the New York City Ballet in 1953. This delightful

ballet glanced back at the Debussy-Nijinsky ballet, but in fact showed two dancers doing class, both so wrapped in narcissism that they almost completely ignore each other, even when dancing a pas de deux. Here the humour was very subtle; in 'The Concert', however, Robbins created wild slapstick humour out of another satire on ballet. Being very self-critical, Robbins abandons more ballets than he completes, but in 1969 he created for the NYCB a beautiful abstract ballet to music by Chopin, 'Dances at a Gathering'.

Harkness Ballet

When Mrs Rebekah Harkness decided to establish a ballet company in America in the sixties, she very wisely broke away from the pattern set by her predecessors. Her plans were in tune with the times, providing for a relatively small company of about thirty dancers, with no corps de ballet, performing nothing but new ballets, and drawing on modern dance as well as ballet choreographers.

The Harkness Ballet was formed in 1964, some of the dancers being taken over from a previous company financed by Mrs Harkness (the Robert Joffrey Ballet), while others were chosen at auditions attended by a very large number of dancers. Before rehearsals started, there were months of classes from a variety of distinguished teachers, to give the company a homogeneous style, and the rehearsals went on for a long time to polish up every detail.

One thing that was very clear at the company's début in Cannes was the verve and youthful freshness of the leading dancers. These young principals stood up well to the comparison with such highly experienced dancers as the guest artists, Erik Bruhn and Marjorie Tallchief. Outstanding among the young dancers were Lawrence Rhodes, Lone Isaksen from Denmark, Helgi Tomasson from Iceland and Brunilda Ruiz (born

Right and opposite John Butler's 'After Eden' with Lawrence Rhodes and Lone Isaksen. This ballet gave exceptional scope to the powerful dramatic talents of its two interpreters (Harkness Ballet, 1967).

in Puerto Rico, but trained at the School of Performing Arts in New York.) After training in Detroit Rhodes had danced in the corps de ballet of the Ballet Russe de Monte Carlo, and had then become a leading dancer in the Robert Joffrey Ballet; he was one of the dancers to move on from this company to the Harkness Ballet in 1964. Lean, intelligent, wiry, he showed a fine presence, and soon established himself as a major artist.

The New York début, crucial for an American company, was delayed until November, 1967, by which time the performances had been polished and the repertoire enlarged to include eighteen ballets in a wide variety of styles, by twelve choreographers: here one could

see Rebekah Harkness moving in the same admirable direction as that taken by Lucia Chase when she launched the great American company, Ballet Theater, in 1940. Nearly all the Harkness ballets used contemporary music, and no less than six had specially commissioned scores—something of great significance in an era in which the development of the art of ballet had been cramped by being almost always based on existing music. Inevitably, the ballets were erratic in quality; and there were too many slick, eclectic works by Brian Macdonald, at this time the company's artistic director. But a number of the pieces gave fine opportunities to the company's splendid principal dancers. Outstanding

among these was 'Monument for a Dead Boy'; here the central role (of a boy whose development is crippled by his family environment) was danced with power and sensitivity by Lawrence Rhodes, one of the greatest of American classically trained actor-dancers, and Lone Isaksen was no less moving as a tender, vulnerable and spiritual girl.

These two were also magnificent in complex roles in John Butler's duo-ballet 'After Eden', in which a mythic story (of what happens to Adam and Eve after their expulsion from Eden) was made into a symbol of tortured, lonely, guilt-ridden relationships between contemporary men and women. Very different in style was 'Requiem for Jimmy Dean', a tough, fast-moving jazz work by Jack Cole, a remarkable teacher and choreographer who added much from Indian dance to American traditions of jazz dance: after scores of rehearsals only six minutes of choreography finally emerged, but the work was impressive even in its unfinished state.

Alvin Ailey contributed a strong dramatic piece, 'Feast of Ashes', based on thr Lorca play 'The House of Bernarda Alba'; originally created for the Joffrey company, it suffered like Tudor ballets in England from changes of cast and lack of attention from the choreographer, but was of exceptional interest.

In the summer of 1968, while the company was working in Monte Carlo, Mrs Harkness appointed the twenty-nine-year-old Lawrence Rhodes as the company's artistic director. This was a fateful event, both for Rhodes—now the youngest director of a major ballet company in the world—and for the company. It was a considerable strain for him, being simultaneously leading dancer and artistic director, but this was a challenge he could hardly refuse.

In 1969 the company gained enormously by the arrival of Benjamin Harkarvy as co-artistic director, thus relieving the impossible strain on Lawrence Rhodes.

MODERN DANCE

Introduction

In the thirties, when Britain was becoming a great creative centre of ballet, great pioneer dancers in America were racing ahead with a new type of dancing: what is now usually known as 'modern dance', though this is rather a misnomer after so many generations of development. Along with jazz, modern dance is one of two great art-forms created by Americans, and both have spread all over the world.

Though to the pioneers of modern dance their work seemed a total revolt against all ballet, the ballet against which they were rebelling was the decadent, sentimental ballet of the last years of the nineteenth century, and their rebellious ideas were similar in many ways to those of Fokine and Nijinsky. The latter, however, did not feel the need to invent a new technique, as did the modern dancers. In fact, the origins of modern dance and twentieth-century ballet were very similar, and each influenced the other.

Isadora Duncan, born in San Francisco in 1878, took ideas from a great many sources, and fused them into a new form of dance which took Europe (and later America) by storm in the early years of this century.

Hard on her heels came another great American pioneer of modern dance, Ruth St Denis. Like Duncan she was influenced by the ideas of the French teacher Delsarte; but instead of ancient Greece she looked to the Orient, and her dances were intended to create an impression of the East without using the highly evolved techniques of Oriental classical dancing. Like Duncan she toured very widely, in Europe and the East as well as in America, and had great success as a solo dancer. But her greatest impact came after her formation, with her partner Ted Shawn, of the Denishawn school in Los Angeles in 1915: it was at this school, and in the various companies associated with it, that the next generation of American modern dancers was formed.

No one technique was taught at Denishawn: Ted Shawn saw it as a 'University of the Dance' at which a variety of types of dancing were taught – above all simplified bare-foot ballet, but also Delsartism and, in the late twenties, German modern dance. The dances produced by the performing groups were invariably exotic: 'East Indian', Aztec, Amerindian, Japanese and so on.

Martha Graham

As a dancer with an overwhelming talent for powerful dramatic expression, and one who longed to develop an American dance with its own technique and its own American themes, Martha Graham was driven to break away from Denishawn in 1923, even though she was dancing leading roles. It was some years before she was able to find her own path. When she first began to give recitals, in 1926, her dances were still largely in the exotic Denishawn manner. But she progressed rapidly in the years that followed, and went on to create major works for decade after decade in a way which is almost without parallel in the history of the dance.

Her work as teacher was no less important and creative than her work as dancer and choreographer. She invented a new technique, of which the characteristic features were contact with the ground, contraction and release of the muscles of the different parts of the body, and an angular, expressionist line, and went on developing it. Year by year she absorbed ideas from other dancers (such as fall-and-recovery from Doris Humphrey), and also from ballet and various Oriental styles, and continued to perfect the line and flow of the move-

ments. Even if she had never created a single dance, her development of the Graham technique would have been enough to immortalize her; in fact her creative achievements in technique and in choreography were inextricably linked in an artistic symbiosis, each essential to the development of the other. What she taught at any time was always related to what she was choreographing at that time.

The year 1930 was a crucial one in her development: she made contact with the greatest achievements of German modern dance when Mary Wigman visited America, and she made indirect contact with the pioneer achievements of Nijinsky when she danced the lead in Massine's version of 'The Rite of Spring'. The following year she created her first large-scale masterpiece, 'Primitive Mysteries', for herself and her students (then all girls). This dance brought together ideas from Wigman, Nijinsky, Ruth St Denis and Ted Shawn, and yet was intensely original, with great consistency of style and ritualistic intensity.

By this time she was not alone: two other dancers who had also been leading dancers in Denishawn, Doris Humphrey and Charles Weidman, had been

moving along a similar path, together evolving a new technique and tackling American themes; Weidman had a great flair for satire, his interpretation of Thurber fables being worthy of Thurber himself, and Doris Humphrey tackled a wide variety of themes. These two had great influence on the next generation of modern dancers; as did Hanya Holm, a pupil of Wigman who sent her to New York in 1931. At first Hanya Holm's teaching and choreography held strictly to Wigman's ideas, but she soon began to develop her own, and influenced American modern dance quite as much as she was influenced by it. Another great pioneer, moving in a parallel path, was Helen Tamiris: she began with a solid grounding in classical ballet, having studied with Fokine, but broke away to found a style and technique that would enable her to create new patterns of movement suited to American themes; in the late twenties, long before anyone else, she was using jazz and spirituals, and tackling themes of social protest. The work of all these five pioneers was centred on New York, and they each kept in touch with what the others were doing and made use of each other's ideas. Out on the West Coast, another great pioneer, Lester Horton, was working on his own in Los Angeles; here he developed his own style and technique, experimenting constantly and taking even more than the others from the East.

But the one who continued to stand out through the years as the archetypal modern dancer was Martha Graham. By the end of the thirties, using both male and female dancers of great talent trained by her, she was able to tackle extremely complex subjects.

The most striking feature of the next few years was Graham's obsession with Greek myths. In dance after dance ('Cave of the Heart', 'Errand into the Maze', 'Night Journey') she gave her own very personal interpretations of the various myths, finding in them something very contemporary as well as something eternal—and always with herself as the tormented central figure. In 'Night Journey', based on the Oedipus myth, the whole dance is built around the tragic figure of Jocasta; and now, with marvellous three-dimensional abstract settings by the great Japanese-American sculptor Isamu Noguchi, she was able to form the movements around and over the décor.

By the end of the forties Martha Graham, after more than three decades on the stage, was no longer dancing with the fire and suppleness of earlier years, and very sensibly began to create works for her company without herself taking part: she now had a group of superb dancers trained by her, and it was a joy to see them being given solo roles worthy of their powers in dances like 'Diversion of Angels', 'Canticles for Innocent Comedians', 'Ardent Song' and 'Seraphic Dialogue'. Each of these had its own unique style and structure.

In 'Diversion of Angels' Martha Graham created for once a work which had no theme, being just pure dancing for its own sake: but what dancing! At this time she was absorbing a great deal of the classical technique at its best, above all through the influence of Tudor. Tudor-style classical classes were taken by Graham dancers, and they developed an exquisite purity of line: not only where one would expect—in classical poses and steps—but also in the Graham patterns; moreover there was a wonderful control of tension, and no strain apparent in hands or neck, no matter how difficult the step. Her dancers became more and more polished, above all in the sixties when she presented pieces like 'Diversion of Angels', danced by such great artists as the Negro dancers Mary Hinkson, Matt Turney, William Louther and Dudley Williams, the exquisite and tiny Japanese dancer

Takako Asakawa, the calm and noble Ethel Winter and the elegant Robert Powell. The result was an overwhelming expression of joy in movement, with Graham patterns which had been invented to express intense feelings and inner conflicts now being used in an abstract way that was in a very real sense classical.

In 'Seraphic Dialogue' Graham achieved a wonderfully simple, ritualistic treatment of the story of Joan of Arc, using four dancers to show four different aspects of the central figure: Joan the Maid, Joan the Warrior, Joan the Martyr and Joan herself. This had décor by Noguchi, made of slender rods of shining tubular steel unlike any previous décor, yet exactly what Graham needed to match her treatment of that theme.

Driven by her daemon, Graham found it hard to continue creating works for her company without herself, and in fact went on to create a number of large-scale works built around her own performances in the central role, with very simplified choreography adjusted to what she could achieve at this stage in her career as a dancer. These performances gave audiences seeing her for the first time on her foreign tours a rather misleading impression of a dancer who had been one of the world's greatest. But she was triumphantly effective in 'Acrobats of God' (1960) in which she satirized in the most devastating way her own methods of work and her relationship with others, as well as sending up the famed Graham charisma. Here her daemon was personified as a ring-master, wonderfully danced and acted by David Wood; but it was Graham herself who stole the show, moving with extraordinary lightness and wit.

As in every period of her life, the works she produced in the sixties, after four decades of creative activity, were erratic in quality; but the best were as good as anything she had ever done.

One of the best was 'Part Real–Part Dream', in which she brought together, in characteristically baffling fashion, a number of different mythical ideas from various periods. There were two fascinating female figures danced by two great Negro artists: a creature of light (portrayed by Matt Turney) and a mysterious dark earth-goddess (Mary Hinkson in long draperies).

Second and Third Generation

The traditions of modern dances as established by Duncan, St Denis, Graham, Humphrey, Weidman, Tamiris, Holm and Horton were such as to encourage creative effort by *all* the young dancers trained by them; choreography was by no means thought of as being confined to a very small number of specialists, as in ballet.

The economic situation of the dancers was also very different from that of ballet dancers. The modern dancers lived to dance, but could not and did not expect to make a living by dancing. Though they had a hard life, with no security, they also enjoyed a great deal of creative freedom, and there was always room for young people to come forward with their own ideas.

In fact these conditions encouraged a wonderful flowering of creativity after the Second World War. From Doris Humphrey's company came the powerful Mexican dancer José Limon; from Martha Graham such extraordinarily varied talents as those of Anna Sokolow, Pearl Lang, Merce Cunningham and Paul Taylor; from Helen Tamiris and Anna Sokolow, the great solo dancer Daniel Nagrin; from Hanya Holm, the great pioneer of abstraction Alwin Nikolais and also Glen Tetley; from Lester Horton, the great Negro choreographer Alvin Ailey. But, whatever their main training, nearly all of these were deeply influenced by Graham and Tudor.

Merce Cunningham

Of all the American modern dance pioneers who combine the roles of leading dancer, sole or chief choreographer and company-director, Merce Cunningham has established himself over the years as the archetypal representative of everything that is exotic, random, cybernetic and what have you. And certainly he has devoted himself, in collaboration with John Cage and various other composers and cybernetic-electronic specialists, as well as the like-minded artist Robert Rauschenberg, to precisely this sort of activity (in which, ideally, robots should move about, under the control of computers applying programs to random numbers, for observation by other robots). But it should not be forgotten that Cunningham established himself at an early stage in his career as a great dancer with a number of virtues rare among male

Above Carolyn Brown in Merce Cunningham's 'Antic Meet'.

Opposite Barbara Lloyd in Cunningham's 'Summerspace'.

dancers (notably sensitivity, lyricism, subtlety, grace, style and poetry); and he has consistently striven to develop such qualities among his dancers, by specially-evolved methods of training–even though these qualities are out of place and of little consequence in the aleatory-electronic world in which he normally works. This contradiction has made his artistic development erratic, but very intriguing.

Though when Cunningham danced leading roles for Graham from 1940 to 1945, he showed a marked gift for the interpretation of dramatic roles requiring strong characterization and the expression of feeling, his flair as choreographer was for elegant, poetic abstraction, and he worked with great success to evolve a technique which would liberate the dancers so that they could move with lightness and poetry in any direction. His success in this admirably creative enterprise was to be seen above all in his own dancing and in that of his principal dancer, Carolyn Brown: tall, slim, elegant, beautiful, with a marvellous extended line, she was the epitome of a new type of classical-modern dancer that was coming to the fore in the late fifties and the sixties.

Another strong influence on Cunningham (as on Cage) was Zen Buddhism; they both attended lectures by Suzuki and read Buddhist books. This helped to give Cunningham a keen awareness of space and time. In a work like 'Summerspace', created in 1958 and danced both by his own company and by the New York City Ballet, he used the whole space of the stage with none of the concentration on the centre previously characteristic of every branch of the theatre. As for time, Cunningham adopted a habit of working with a stopwatch, and creating the choreography in total independence of the music; the importance of the watch was that he could arrange the dancing to end at the same time as the music.

Cage and Cunningham were two pioneers of the Happening, as well as of the aleatory (chance) thing, and in 'Variations V' Cunningham and his cyberneticians combined together the Happening, the aleatory thing, the cybernetic thing, film and still projections and a great deal of fast dancing in what looked and sounded like an all-out attempt to blind the spectator with science. The stage was covered with thin vertical rods, fitted with electronic equipment so that they responded to the proximity of dancers, and in the orchestra pit two electronic engineers arranged for impulses from these rods to trigger off sounds of many kinds.

In many items like this one had the feeling, rightly or wrongly, that Cunningham was being used by colleagues seeking a chance to try out their ideas. But there were other items–notably

'Field Dances' and 'How to Pass, Kick, Run and Fall'–in which Cunningham brought together all kinds of new ideas and shaped them, in accord with his intensively serious ideals of poetic dancing, into witty new syntheses.

Paul Taylor

Paul Taylor is a large, friendly, relaxed person, quite unlike the archetypal modern-dance choreographer, who tends to be highly strung and Angst-ridden. His main training was at the Juilliard School of Music, where he learned Graham modern dance and also studied ballet with Tudor, and he later trained under Graham and Tudor in their own schools; in fact, he brings together modern-dance and ballet traditions in a way very characteristic of his generation. When he was only twenty-four, he formed his own company, and staged a work of extraordinary originality, 'Three Epitaphs', which was quite unlike anything by his mentors Graham and Tudor and, in a macabre way, wildly

funny. It was based on some extraordinary folk music (an ancestor of jazz), once performed at weddings and funerals in the Deep South, with an unforgettable growling violence. To match this music Taylor imagined some zombies covered entirely in black, with mirrors on the costumes reflecting flickers of light over a gloomy stage, drooping about the stage in sinister and wonderfully funny patterns. Later, from 1955 to 1961, Taylor had the invaluable experience of dancing in the Graham company as a leading soloist, while he continued to create works with his own company.

In the years that followed, Taylor began to concentrate on a curious sort of neo-classicism, using classical music and simplified and distorted versions of classical ballet steps. These works lacked the power and originality of his early satirical pieces, and in fact he seemed to be moving up a blind alley–apart from the wonderfully inventive 'Hand Dance' in 'Piece Period', in which the dancers moved with a prim formality and stiff,

mad little movements, in a devastating satire of social dances like the minuet.

Another path that seemed to be a blind alley was what might be called Cage-Cunninghamism–as in the dance 'Insects and Heroes' (1961). This had all the canonical ingredients, including a far-out post-Webernite score, a line of dancers switching on light-bulbs on their heads, and a creature in a strange tubular costume, covered in spikes–a costume which hardly allowed her to walk, much less dance. This work was so much in the modish Cage-Cunningham vein that at times it might almost have been a burlesque; but there were no clear signs of satirical intent.

In 1966 Taylor broke through into a new world with a large-scale masterpiece, 'Orbs', which was unlike anything that he or anyone else had done. Although it used classical music, there was none of the clash between the patterns of movement and the music which is characteristic of the dances created by modern dancers using old

*Opposite Merce Cunningham's
'Variations V'.*

*Above Martha Graham as the old Judith
in her 'Legend of Judith' (Martha Graham
Company).*

Right and opposite Taylor's 'Scudorama'
with Elizabeth Walton and
Dan Waggoner.

music; and Taylor broke clean away from his rather tame earlier efforts at neo-classicism. Using some powerful and mysterious late Beethoven quartets, themselves far ahead of their time, Taylor composed a large-scale work, lasting two acts, in which he responded with great sensitivity to the surging dynamism of the music, building up structures which matched each change in its mood.

Alvin Ailey

Unlike the Negro slaves of Latin America, those of the United States were treated as mere chattels and deprived of any sort of human dignity, and so lost nearly all their rich African heritage of music and dance. But that did not stop them from dancing and making music, and they took the arts of their white masters and developed them in a great many original ways, often distorting them as forms of protest. The great creative achievements of Negro artists in spirituals, blues and jazz are well known for their freshness, power, originality and spontaneity; the corresponding Negro achievements in modern dance and jazz dance came later, but they were no less impressive.

Alvin Ailey's achievements in this field are unique. Not only has he brought to the stage the great riches of the American Negro's cultural heritage: he has succeeded in carrying out his bold and creative plan of establishing a true repertory company that brings together the work of many different choreog-

raphers in a variety of Negro and non-Negro styles, instead of staging only his own dances; and he has built up a company which gives great opportunities to Negro dancers, and indeed includes some of the finest modern dancers in the world: the powerful and intense William Louther, the sensitive Dudley Williams, the tall and assured Judith Jamison, with her Masai profile, the febrile, brilliant Puerto Rican Miguel Godreau, and the classically beautiful Consuelo Atlas, with her depth of feeling and pure classical line. He also gives fine opportunities to great dancers of other races, such as Joyce Trisler and the Japanese artist Takako Asakawa. His own dances, drawing together ideas from Horton, Graham, Humphrey, Holm and Tudor, nevertheless show a style which is very much his own, and include some of the finest achievements of American modern dance; apart from creating for his own company, he has composed works for companies such as the Harkness and the Joffrey Ballets. He presents his dances with great attention to detail and remarkable theatrical flair: characteristically, he has had the lighting created for them by two of the greatest artists in the field, Nicola Cernovich and Thomas Skelton.

Quite early in his career, in 1960, he created a masterpiece, 'Revelations', which exhibited a perfection of detail and a solidity of construction rare in modern dance or ballet, and a special, additional quality of ecstatic, magical freshness and simplicity, very charac-

teristic of the Negro spirituals on which it was based. Many others had used spirituals before Ailey; but he brought to them exactly the right qualities of temperament and inspiration needed to do them full justice. However often one sees this work, it never loses its power to enchant: beneath its apparent simplicity it is a work of great sophistication and subtlety. In the great procession of the middle section, the dancers move in broad, simple, lyrical rhythms; the girls in their wide white skirts, the men carrying white banners and branches, and all swept along by the surging dynamism of the music; but each dancer or group moves in a different relationship to the music, and the choreographic counterpoint is in fact very complex.

He is very versatile: 'Hermit Songs', for example, are dances for one man, full of a nobility and mystical aspiration which could belong to any race; 'Quintet' is a highly sophisticated mixture of gay, mocking, exuberant satires on commercialized sex and solos of passionate Negro protest. Ailey has continuously widened his repertoire with admirable judgment, setting alongside his own dances works by leading choreographers, both white and Negro. One masterpiece that he introduced was Anna Sokolow's 'Rooms', based like a number of her works on jazz music; the Ailey dancers brought out with depth and understanding its powerful interpretation of the despair of individuals living solitary lives in the big city. Variety was also added to the repertoire by a number

*Below Alvin Ailey's 'Revelations'; the
Procession scene leading to the river
(Alvin Ailey Company).*

*Opposite Lester Horton's 'The Beloved'
with James Truitte (Alvin Ailey
Company).*

*Next page Alvin Ailey's 'Revelations';
the opening scene (Alvin Ailey
Company).*

of works by the Negro choreographer Talley Beatty, in which he showed his extraordinary gift for giving expression to the violent feelings of Negro protest, by means of abstract, fast and tensely dynamic dancing, with a strong emphasis on ballet steps used in new combinations which fitted the jazz music. Then there was the fascinating 'Prodigal Prince' (1968) in which Trinidad-born Geoffrey Holder used his studies of Haitian Voodoo to construct a complex dramatic work showing the strange gods (part African, part Christian) which take possession of Voodoo initiates.

By his skill and imagination in drawing on the rich heritage of American Negro culture and in giving opportunities to Negro dancers, and also by his admirable policy of building up a broad and well-balanced repertoire, Ailey is able to attract a wide range of spectators in a great many countries; in London he even played for *two* long seasons in 1964-5, establishing his company as a part of the London theatrical scene rather as the Ballet-Russe companies did in the thirties. At the Congress of African Art in Dakar in 1967, and during its long tour of East and West Africa, his company made a deep impression on many Africans, and its performances are likely to have a long-lasting influence on the development of African theatrical dance as it becomes more sophisticated and urbanized.

Soviet Ballet

INTRODUCTION

In the quantity of ballet performed and the number of spectators, the Soviet Union is far ahead of any other country. There are no less than thirty-four full-time professional ballet companies in thirty-one cities, spread out over the largest country in the world. Apart from professional ballet, there are over two million amateurs who study ballet, and sometimes perform. Whereas in most countries ballet appeals to a minority audience, in the Soviet Union it has a mass appeal.

There is something paradoxical about the vast popularity of ballet in the Soviet Union and the great seriousness with which it is regarded by a state which was established by the first successful proletarian revolution. For the ballet taken over at the Revolution by the workers' state was very much a court art, under the control of a court official appointed by the Tsar, performed at the Imperial Theatres by members of the Imperial household, before supremely elegant and aristocratic audiences. By a cruel irony of fate the great Diaghilev ballets were not part of the heritage taken over by Soviet ballet because they were not in the repertoire of the Imperial Theatres at the time of the Revolution. The repertoire taken over in fact consisted of 'La Fille Mal Gardée (known as 'Vain Precautions'), two Perrot ballets ('Giselle' and 'Esmeralda'), a good many Petipa ballets, the Petipa-Ivanov ballet 'Swan Lake', the Ivanov ballet 'The Nutcracker', and some pre-Diaghilev Fokine ballets (notably 'Chopiniana', known in the West as 'Les Sylphides' because Diaghilev chose to rename it).

KIROV BALLET

St Petersburg was the cosmopolitan and sophisticated capital of Imperial Russia; the court was here, and here, under the eye of the Tsar, at the Maryinsky, the best dancers and the best ballets were assembled. The Maryinsky company suffered heavily in the aftermath of the Revolution. Almost none of the great dancers and teachers could see any future for their highly refined art in socialist Russia, and left the country: and many Russians said that ballet was bound to disappear, for it would have no place in the new socialist world that was being constructed. But ballet did survive, thanks to Lunacharsky, the cultured and sensitive man who as Commissar for Education had charge of the theatrical arts, and it was soon developing as fast as all the other arts. In the twenties men like Vakhtangov, Tairov

and Meyerhold gave the Soviet Union the most advanced theatre in the world, and men like Eisenstein and Pudovkin led the world in film-making. Petrograd/Leningrad was the home of a great number of experiments in dancing, paralleling the avant-garde trends in the other arts: as in Germany there was barefoot dancing, near nudity, expressionism, constructivism, 'plastique', erotic Orientalism, acrobatics and many other forms of free dance. By far the most important of the innovators in choreography was Fyodor Lopukhov, a brilliant character dancer who graduated into the Maryinsky in 1905, became its chief choreographer in 1920 and its artistic director in 1922; he continued to direct it, through an exciting period of development, up to 1930; and he also directed it in 1944-7 and 1955-8.

Opposite 'Giselle' performed by the Kirov Ballet, with Natalia Makarova as Giselle.

Above Alexander Pushkin, the great teacher of male dancing at the Kirov.

Lopukhov's great achievements as director of the ballet company of the Leningrad State Theatre of Opera and Ballet (once called Maryinsky, and called Kirov after 1935) were many-sided. He had great knowledge of, and respect for, the classical traditions of the company and he preserved them with the utmost care, faithfully maintaining the choreography of the ballet, and producing them in a way which brought them to life, while at the same time preserving the purest and most noble traditions of dancing in both company and school; in fact he established the Kirov on a course which it has maintained to this day, resisting the common tendency in the Soviet Union to regard choreography as something ephemeral which can and ought to be changed continually.

Though most of the leading teachers (notably Legat) had left, there were two fine dancers who became great teachers: Vladimir Ponomaryev and Agrippina Vaganova, who became the leading teachers of male and female dancers respectively. Thanks to their work, and that of other teachers, such as Maria Romanova, the school began to produce excellent dancers just as it had done before the Revolution, and from 1925 onwards it was graduating such great artists as Semyonova, Yermolayev, Chabukiani, Konstantin Sergueyev and the incomparable Galina Ulanova (daughter of Romanova). With fine classical dancers, admirably produced by Lopukhov, the classics could shine out with all their old glory.

Alongside this preservation of the company's rich heritage, Lopukhov introduced new ideas into its work with intelligence, imagination and good taste. Leontiev had staged his own version of 'Petrushka' in 1920, and Lopukhov staged his version of 'The Firebird' in 1921, thus adding to the repertoire at least some Diaghilevian elements. Fokine had left Russia in 1918, so it was not possible to revive the original choreography. Lopukhov also introduced training in acrobatics and free dance into the school, and in 1923 he staged a very advanced and important ballet, 'Tanzsymphonia', the first abstract-symbolic symphonic ballet, ante-dating by nearly a decade the symphonic ballets with which Massine made such a great stir in the thirties while working for the Ballet-Russe companies in the West.

*Left Natalia Makarova as Giselle and
Yuri Soloviev as Albrecht in 'Giselle'
Act II (Kirov Ballet).*

*Below Irina Kolpakova as Aurora in 'The
Sleeping Beauty' (Kirov Ballet).*

*Right Irina Kolpakova as Aurora and
Vladilen Semyonov as the Prince in 'The
Sleeping Beauty' (Kirov Ballet).*

New ballets demanded new techniques from the dancers: in Lopukhov's 'Ice Maiden' (1927) he introduced some beautiful high lifts, inspired partly by the acrobatics which had become part of Soviet ballet, and Vaganova developed ways of teaching dancers to perform these lifts; she also further developed the freedom and ease of movement characteristic of the Petersburg school of ballet.

But the artistic climate changed very greatly in Russia in the thirties; this was a sad and terrible period, when new ideas in all the arts were suspect, and millions of people disappeared into labour camps. Soviet ballet, forced to abandon expressionism, symbolism, abstraction and all the other new ideas, moved back towards Petipa and the large-scale three-act Romantic ballet with conventional Petipa-type choreography.

Fortunately Soviet choreographers found a way of coming to terms with the new artistic climate by basing their ballets on romantic stories by great writers of the past, and making considerable use of character dance. One such ballet was 'The Fountain of Bakhchisaraï', based on a Pushkin poem. This had a very romantic story of the abduction of Maria, the daughter of a Polish prince, by the Tartar Khan Girei, and the killing of Maria by Zarema, the 'star' of Girei's harem. This was simply and intelligently staged by Rotislav Zakharov in 1934 as a kind of mime play with dances. This was hardly choreography in the real sense of the word—it was dramatic production with the addition of conventional dances which might have belonged to any ballet, and it really belonged to the pre-Fokine era—but the ballet had its own theatrical power and its central role (Maria) was superbly acted and danced by Ulanova. The last act took the form of a series of exciting character dances by the Tartar warriors.

The masterpiece of this neo-Romantic style of ballet production was 'Romeo and Juliet', staged by Leonid Lavrovsky in 1940 with music by Prokofiev. This was a triumphant success, and has become world-famous as the supreme achievement of Soviet ballet; in fact new versions of it have been staged in a great many countries.

Though Lavrovsky had clearly learned a lot from the success of Zakharov in 'The Fountain of Bakhchisaraï', he went even further than Zakharov in giving detailed attention to the text of the literary source of his ballet, trying to find an equivalent to Shakespeare's actual words in the details of the mimed action and the dancing.

What stood out above all in this ballet was Lavrovsky's superb production and his convincing use of mime. The big

Right Galina Ulanova, greatest of all Soviet ballerinas, and now ballet mistress of the Bolshoi Ballet.

Below Robert Helpmann's 'Hamlet', with Rudolf Nureyev as Hamlet and Lynn Seymour as Ophelia.

Opposite top Alla Osipenko as the Mistress of the Copper Mountain in Yuri Grigorovich's 'The Stone Flower' (Kirov Ballet).

Opposite below 'Raymonda' with Irina Kolpakova in the title role (Kirov Ballet).

fight scenes were magnificent, but equally so were a great many of the nuances of the action, and Lavrovsky used mime very skilfully to suggest the characters of the protagonists, and their changes of mood. No less striking was the musicality of his arrangements of steps in the dances; though hardly expressive in themselves, and showing no understanding of the great advances in dance-imagery achieved by Fokine and others, the patterns of steps were, so to speak, neutral, and the fine artists performing them (above all Ulanova) were able to pour a wealth of feeling into them.

Another effective ballet in this same tradition of neo-Romanticism based on works of literature was Lopukhov's 'Taras Bulba' (1940), based on a novel by Gogol about Cossacks and their fight with Polish invaders. This boasted some magnificent character-dancing in a style based on Ukrainian folk-dancing, but enlarged with the full resources of the classical technique.

Though the Kirov lost its best dancers and teachers to the Bolshoi from the twenties onwards, it maintained its traditions very well. The school still had fine teachers, and produced magnificent dancers, while the great dancer Konstantin

Sergueyev, who took over as artistic director from Lopukhov, carried on the latter's splendid work in the same way.

The Lopukhov-Sergueyev production of 'Giselle', with Makarova in the title role, is a miracle of good taste, authenticity, musicality and richness of detail. Not only is there an impeccable sense of period, with all the dancers suggesting the old French style, making their movements rounded and gentle rather than broadly extended in the Russian manner: there is a creative quality in the production which makes the ballet spring to life as a work of art, not a museum piece.

Musically it is precisely controlled, so as to give full value to every detail of the choreography, in a way seen in no other version. The slow passages are much slower than in other versions, while the fast passages are up to full speed; and even within a passage in one basic tempo there are subtle variations in pace corresponding to changes in the choreography. As for Makarova, she has all the qualities of an ideal Maryinsky/Kirov ballerina: long and thoroughly trained at the school, and coached by Ulanova, she established her own interpretation at her very first performance of the role (at Covent Garden in 1961), and has since perfected it, making it a masterpiece of poetry and lyricism. Her Act I Giselle is very shy, rather serious, and very vulnerable; but by subtle touches she makes clear her overwhelming passion for Albrecht. One of her greatest achievements in both acts is to fill out the movements at the very slow tempi in such a way as to do full justice to them, and so build up a choreographic image of Giselle's passionate simplicity.

The Kirov production of 'The Sleeping Beauty' is also magnificent, keeping much more faithfully to the original than any version performed in the West. In the title role Alla Sizova is outstanding: fresh, spontaneous, charming, with wonderful elevation. The role is also well suited to the talents of Irina Kolpakova, who has a strong technique and

quiet charm, though without the magical radiance of Makarova, Sizova or Osipenko. Alla Osipenko is a very individual and exotic artist belonging to the same generation as Kolpakova, but very different in style. She was made a ballerina in 1954 after a stunning performance of Odette-Odile in 'Swan Lake', deploying her unique and fascinating line, with long supple legs curving upwards towards an ecstatic infinity, and making noble and mysterious poetry out of the choreography. The Kirov production of 'Swan Lake' is tasteful and intelligent: it retains most of the poetic Ivanov choreography in the 'swan' acts (Acts II and IV), but changes the stage patterns in a way that is true to the spirit of the ballet (making them rather more complex, with various groups of swans moving independently in different phrasing). The main weakness of the production is the happy ending.

In 1957 the thirty-year old Kirov choreographer Yuri Grigorovich made a name for himself by staging a new version of the Lavrovsky ballet 'The Stone Flower', a three-act ballet based on folk-tales of the Urals. Much of Grigorovich's choreography was very conventional in the usual Soviet neo-Petipan manner, but he created some very effective exotic movements for the great Osipenko, exploiting her gift for strange soaring leg and arm movements and her flair for the mysterious and magical.

'The Stone Flower' was such a success with audiences that Grigorovich was asked to stage it for the Bolshoi in 1959, and in due course he was appointed chief choreographer and then artistic director of the Bolshoi Ballet.

In 1958 the Kirov took on a young male dancer who looked as if he would develop into an artist comparable in every way to its finest ballerinas – Rudolf Nureyev. But he left the company in 1961, and so did not become the company's leading danseur, as he certainly would have done had he stayed.

Instead, it was Yuri Soloviev who went to the top. Purely as a dancer, he has outstanding gifts: there are very few male dancers in the world who can equal him in purity of line, elevation, ease and fluidity. His acting ability is limited, however, and his face has a round, slightly girlish cast which is ill-suited to the traditional classical roles. But he looked magnificently heroic and virile as the wartime leader of the defenders of Leningrad in a rather naive ballet by Igor Belsky, 'Leningrad Symphony'.

In the late sixties a great young male dancer emerged, worthy of the finest traditions of the company: the noble and powerful Mikhail Barishnikov. One of the finest of Kirov danseurs is Valeri Panov, who combines a powerful and versatile dramatic talent with charm, panache and a superb technique.

BOLSHOI BALLET

Towards the end of the nineteenth century the prestige and standards of the Bolshoi Ballet in Moscow had fallen to a very low ebb: it did not reflect the great achievements of the Maryinsky, and the Directorate of the Imperial Theatres considered closing it down. But the outstanding Bolshoi dancer Vassili Tikhomirov, after two years of taking 'perfection classes' in St Petersburg, returned to the Bolshoi in 1893; soon afterwards he began to give classes, and rapidly established a magnificent tradition of male dancing.

The other great stimulus to the Bolshoi came from the work there of the ballet-master Alexander Gorsky in the early years of this century. Working on new versions of Maryinsky ballets, he strove energetically to make the action more interesting and convincing, and tended to change the choreography to some extent; working on 'Swan Lake', he staged no less than five successive versions. He did a great deal to revitalize the Bolshoi; but unfortunately he also established a tradition of constant and thorough-going reworking of the classics which has persisted to this day. This strange attitude to the work of great choreographers of the past is rather like that of the English actors of the seventeenth and eighteenth centuries, who 'modernized' the texts of the Shakespeare plays in which they appeared, and thereby destroyed the poetic qualities which gave the plays their greatness.

When the capital was moved to Moscow after the October Revolution, it was quite natural that the Soviet government should want to make the Bolshoi the leading ballet in the country, and so during the twenties, thirties and forties many of the finest of the Kirov dancers and teachers were brought to Moscow; moreover the finest Kirov productions were re-staged for the Bolshoi by Kirov choreographers, including 'The Fountain of Bakhchisaraï' (staged in Moscow in 1936, two years after its creation in Leningrad) and 'Romeo and

Opposite Nicolai Fadeyechev as Prince Siegfried, Maya Plisetskaya as Odette and Vladimir Levashov as the Evil Magician in the Bolshoi Ballet's version of 'Swan Lake'.

Left Rimma Karelskaya as the Tsar-Maiden in Alexander Radunsky's version of 'The Humpbacked Horse'. Photo taken in the foyer of the Royal Opera House, Covent Garden (Bolshoi Ballet).

Juliet', staged in Moscow in 1946, six years after the Leningrad production.

These efforts succeeded brilliantly. The Bolshoi developed into one of the world's greatest companies, with magnificent productions of 'Giselle' and the best Soviet ballets, and with a school producing a stream of young ballerinas, the best of whom had a style which was quite as pure and poetic as the best of the Maryinsky/Kirov ballerinas, as well as magnificent male dancers with a fire and virility that owed as much to the Bolshoi's own fine traditions as they did to those of the Kirov.

The Bolshoi is to be seen at its greatest in 'Giselle'; for here the traditional choreography has been retained in all its rich detail, thus giving splendid opportunities to the company's splendid dancers.

Though originally created for the Kirov, Lavrovsky's production of 'Romeo and Juliet' suits the Bolshoi so perfectly that one would swear it had been created with this company in mind. Ever since Gorsky the Bolshoi has maintained a tradition of powerful realistic acting, and its dancers lend great individuality to their interpretation of the various parts; in the fighting scenes, the Bolshoi's strong traditions of character dancing find an exciting outlet. And for

nearly two decades the Bolshoi had the incomparable Ulanova, who created the role of Juliet, dancing this role to perfection.

The Bolshoi's production of 'Swan Lake', much influenced by the various Gorsky productions, is much less satisfactory. Nevertheless enough of Ivanov's great choreography remains to give fine opportunities to the Bolshoi's great ballerinas.

Ulanova was one of those very rare artists who enriched the classical tradition while maintaining all its greatest virtues. Her musicality was such that she seemed to dance the music instead of dancing to the music. Everything she did was marvellously spontaneous and sincere, so that each performance was a new experience both for her and the audience. Her interpretations were intensely original, yet always seemed so right and inevitable that while she was on stage it was impossible to imagine them being done in any other way. Her sense of line was so exquisite that she was always able to look elegant and beautiful even though her physique was far from ideal (her neck being rather short). Her technique was strong, but she used it with such naturalness and artistry that one was never aware of it. Where she stood out above all was in her ability to

*Opposite Yuri Grigorovich's version of
'The Nutcracker' with Ekaterina
Maximova as Masha, Vladimir Levashov
(Drosselmeyer) as the Conjurer and Alla
Shcherbinina as the Nutcracker Doll
(Bolshoi Ballet).*

*Below Yuri Grigorovich's version of
'Spartacus' with Maris Liepa as Crassus
in two leaps (Bolshoi Ballet).*

combine movements into a seamless whole, each one flowing into the next with magical inevitability. This legato flow was seen at its finest in the 'Swan Lake' pas de deux in which she kept every part of her body in movement the whole time, with the phrasing of hands, head and feet integrated in the most subtle and moving manner: her interpretation of this pas de deux has become standard throughout the world.

After retiring as a dancer in 1962 Ulanova became ballet-mistress of the Bolshoi, making a great contribution to Russian ballet by coaching outstanding young dancers, and young stars like Maximova, Besmertnova and Makarova (of the Kirov) owe an incalculable debt to her. One of the most remarkable features of the Bolshoi (and of other Soviet companies) is the very great care given to the coaching of young dancers: it sometimes happens that a dancer works on a great classical role for a year or more before she makes her début in it.

The prima ballerina who took over from Ulanova at the Bolshoi, Maya Plisetskaya, is very different in style, background and temperament. Had she been born in the United States she would certainly have become a modern dancer, and in fact she has an extraordinary gift for balletic expressionism, moving her arms and back through strange positions which depart a long way from the classical canon and are yet full of expressive vitality.

Her highly individual and magnetic personality is seen most clearly in 'The Dying Swan', the solo choreographed by Fokine for Pavlova, and her Odette has much the same qualities as her Dying Swan. Her long thin face and lustrous eyes project each nuance of feeling; arching her head and shoulders further back than one would have thought possible, she creates an entirely individual Odette. The powerful arm-gestures suggesting wingbeats have none of the lyricism one expects in this role: instead, they have an exotic and expressionist violence more suited to Fokine's Firebird; and her movements have the impetuous freedom and dynamism characteristic of the old Bolshoi school, but carried to the nth degree. All this makes nonsense of the theme of the ballet–this Odette would make mincemeat of the wicked magician–but it is exhilarating and spell-binding. Sometimes her movements are ugly or clumsy, sometimes wonderfully subtle and sensitive: but always she is uniquely herself. Like all Soviet dancers she has been greatly influenced by Ulanova; she worked on Odette-Odile for five years before dan-

cing it for the first time in 1961, and then showed an interpretation very different from Ulanova's.

Another great Bolshoi dancer of Plisetskaya's generation is Raïssa Struchkova. She has great vitality and warmth of temperament, dramatic ability, and a wonderfully simple, direct and natural approach to roles like Giselle, Juliet and Maria (in 'The Fountain of Bakhchisaraï').

The Bolshoi has been producing great male dancers for the whole of this century, and those coming to the fore in the sixties included three artists of the very highest talent, all sharply contrasted in temperament. Vladimir Vasiliev has such power, such elevation and such ease in the most difficult feats that he appears more as a force of nature than a merely human dancer. Mikhail Lavrovsky, no less perfect in technique, stands out as the beau ideal of the danseur noble, giving

perfect masculine grace and elegance to every movement, and acting with all the combination of power, dignity and restraint characteristic of the greatest traditions of classical ballet. And there is another magnificent danseur noble, Yuri Vladimirov. No other company has such a phenomenal trio of male dancers.

Also to emerge in the sixties were some great classical ballerinas with all the purity of line and elegant poetry of movement characteristic of the Kirov, outstanding among them being Besmertnova and Sorokina. By this time the Bolshoi was by far the biggest company in the world, with about two hundred and fifty dancers and two big theatres at its disposal – the old Bolshoi and the enormous new Palace of Congresses in the Kremlin.

Opposite Nikita Dolgushin in the 'Corsaire' pas de deux (Bolshoi Ballet).

Above Elena Riabinkina with Alexander Begak in a pas de deux from 'Raymonda' (Bolshoi Ballet).

Rudolf Nureyev

Right Rudolf Nureyev and Nadia Nerina
in the 'Black Swan' pas de deux from
'Swan Lake'.

Opposite Margot Fonteyn and Rudolf
Nureyev.

Since the magical appearance of Nijinsky before the First World War, no male dancer has captured the imagination of millions as Rudolf Nureyev has done. Like Rudolf Valentino, like Marilyn Monroe, like the Beatles, he has become the incarnation of a modern myth.

Part of his unique appeal is due to his dancing: he is beyond question one of the finest dancers in the world. But he is no better than a number of others, and he has developed certain regrettable faults of style (like a habit of trying to suggest passion by keeping his mouth open) which are unworthy of a great

classical dancer. Moreover his range is limited: he is very much a 'star' rather than an interpretative artist, creating his familiar image in almost every role, and he is baffled by roles such as 'Petrushka', which do not fit this image. Other male dancers have techniques quite as good as his, show no faults of style, and are more versatile; but Nureyev has unique charisma and sex appeal, generated by his exotic, high-cheekboned Tartar face, his arrogant, rebellious individualism, and his cat-like ease, grace and fluidity of movement, displayed to advantage even in a simple run across the stage.

At the Kirov School he joined the class of the great teacher Alexander Pushkin. There he started at a great disadvantage, having had far less training than the others in the class; but he made such rapid progress that he became the leading student of his generation and was given the chance of dancing leading roles in school performances of no less than nine full-length classics.

Soon after joining the Kirov company he became a soloist, dancing the leading roles in 'La Bayadère', 'Le Corsaire', 'Don Quixote', 'Laurencia' and 'Taras Bulba', but was frustrated by the

same problem that troubles the soloists in all big companies: insufficient opportunities of performing. The Kirov, giving fifteen performances a month – a relatively high figure – had fifteen male soloists and twenty premiers danseurs, so that any one artist could only hope to take a leading role about five times a year. He aroused official disapproval, too, by his very independent, undisciplined behaviour. The quality of his talent was recognized, and when Sergueyev, artistic director of the Kirov, selected dancers for a visit by the company to Paris and other cities of the West in 1961, he rehearsed Nureyev to take over his own roles.

In Paris Nureyev made a striking impact, and would no doubt have done the same in London; but he found that instead of going there he was being sent to Moscow, and he thereupon decided to leave the company, and make his career in the West. His escape at Le Bourget

airport and his successful request for political asylum launched him on a new career in the midst of a blaze of publicity which has accompanied him ever since.

Immediately after 'choosing freedom' Nureyev joined the Grand Ballet du Marquis du Cuevas, and danced with this company for a year. Meanwhile, offers came to him from all over the world. He first met Margot Fonteyn at a gala which she organized in London, and this began a partnership which became one of the striking features of international ballet in the sixties. He developed a specially close relationship with two companies, the Royal Ballet and the Vienna State Opera Ballet, dancing for both companies quite often and also arranging versions of the classic ballets for these companies – including 'Raymonda', the 'Act of the Shades' of 'La Bayadère', and 'The Nutcracker' for the Royal Ballet and 'Swan Lake' for the Vienna Staatsoper; but he also staged ballets and danced for a good many other companies around the world.

As a dancer Nureyev was still immature, both technically and artistically, when he made his famous leap into the arms of the French policeman at Le Bourget airport: this was only to be expected, for he had crammed into three years what normally takes double the time at least. When he first danced Albrecht in 'Giselle' at Covent Garden in 1962 his interpretation had a number of serious flaws: his mime, for example, was weak and poorly projected. But his dancing was outstanding, and his dramatic ability developed rapidly as he took over various dramatic roles. He was outstanding when he took over a great contemporary role in which he was perfectly cast – that of the outsider hero of 'Monument for a Dead Boy', performed by the Dutch National Ballet.

His productions of his own versions of Kirov ballets made it clear that he has a wonderful memory, and a fine understanding of the classical technique which enables him to give help to his chosen ballerinas. When he staged 'The Nutcracker' for the Royal Ballet, carrying still further the idea, already developed in the Kirov version, of making the whole main part of the ballet a dream of little Clara (and having Clara danced by a grown-up ballerina instead of a little girl), he showed a good deal of intelligence in developing a consistent story line. His attempts at creating new patterns of steps – patterns which he thought of as 'English' rather than Kirovian – were much less effective than his versions of Kirov patterns, often cutting right across the music; but he produced a wonderful performance from Merle Park, around whom he created the role of Clara.

Denmark

Tiny Denmark shares with mighty Russia the credit for preserving the great traditions of classical ballet through the decadence of the second half of the nineteenth century right up to modern times. There are two reasons for this. One is that Denmark had a Royal ballet, supported by court patronage and therefore resistant to the whims of popular taste; the other is that in the middle years of the nineteenth century Danish ballet became outstanding under the influence of a great choreographer and teacher whose name was August Bournonville, and the Danes were proud to carry on the Bournonville tradition after his death.

Bournonville's 'La Sylphide', though based on an earlier ballet by Filippo Taglioni which inaugurated the romantic era in ballet, has different music from the Taglioni version and shows Bournonville's special talents in every detail—such as the delicate humour in the role of the Sylphide, the importance given to male classical dancing, the dynamism of the Scottish character dances, and the marvellously horrible acting part of Madge the Witch. This ballet has always been a jewel of the Danish repertoire, like 'Giselle' in the Russian repertoire, and the three principal roles—James, the Sylphide and Madge—have always been favourites of Danish dancers, just as Giselle and Albrecht were and are favourites in Russia.

'Et Folkesagn' (A Folk Tale) shows a different aspect of Bournonville's talent, for it is a medieval legend, with two admirably grotesque male figures, Diderik and Viderik. Then there are the beautiful sequences of pure classical

Previous page left The Royal Danish Ballet in Harald Lander's 'Etudes'.

Previous page right Erik Bruhn as Siegfried and Nadia Nerina as Odette in the 'White Swan' pas de deux from Act I of 'Swan Lake'.

Right Erik Bruhn.

Opposite left Toni Lander.

Opposite right Erik Bruhn demonstrating a point to Austin Bennet in a production of Bournonville's 'Napoli' (Royal Ballet).

dancing in the dancing class in 'Konservatoriet'—showing the French school as taught by Vestris in Paris in Bournonville's youth—and the brilliant passages of dancing in classical and demi-caractère style in scenes from 'Napoli' and 'Flower Festival in Genzano', with fast and very complex beats and the crisp and exciting patterns of leaps for both male and female dancers. These two Bournonville suites have become well-known in many different countries through productions by Danish dancers and balletmasters for local companies.

Though there was no renaissance in creativity in Denmark as there was in Russia, there was a great improvement in the standard of performance of the Bournonville ballets after the appointment of Hans Beck as ballet-master in 1894, and this continued after his retirement in 1915. The company was then fortunate in having a strong, creative director in Harald Lander from 1932 to 1951; during the forties and fifties it had,

thanks to Lander, leading dancers who continued the company's finest traditions while widening their range to include roles in Russian ballets.

Two of these dancers were appointed to leading positions in 1942; Margot Lander, Harald Lander's first wife, was wonderfully noble, simple and moving as 'Giselle', while Børge Ralov could make even a relatively simple role like Gennaro in 'Napoli' come to life with his fire, dynamism and strong acting ability. The next great dancer to emerge was Margrethe Schanne. She was incomparable as the Sylphide, making the most of its fey humour and gentle romanticism: it was a sad day for Danish ballet when she gave her farewell performance in this role in 1966.

The greatest of all the danseurs nobles to emerge in Denmark after the Second World War was Erik Bruhn. He became a soloist in 1949, and showed outstanding ability in all the classical roles, with perfect line, magnificent presence and characteristically Danish dramatic

power. Unfortunately for Denmark, he chose to spend a great deal of his time dancing outside Denmark, and became one of the leading members of a small group of international stars that also included Nureyev.

Between the wars and after the Second World War the Danish repertoire was strengthened by the addition of the major classics of the international repertoire; 'Les Sylphides', 'Giselle', 'Swan Lake', 'Petrushka' and so on. The one Danish ballet to take its place alongside these old and new classics was Harald Lander's ballet 'Etudes', designed to show the whole range of classical training, and cosmopolitan rather than Bournonvillean in style (though clearly inspired in part by the ballet class in Bournonville's 'Konservatoriet'). Here Lander composed the leading female roles to suit the talents of Margot Lander and Toni Lander.

In the late sixties the Royal company suffered from a lack of ballerinas of the stature of Margot Lander and Margrethe

Schanne, but it had some admirable male dancers–notably Flemming Flindt, who became director of the company at the very young age of thirty in 1966, and the short but brilliant Niels Kehlet, with his perfect technique, great speed and elevation, delightful sense of humour and magnetic personality.

Danish dancing has been greatly helped since 1952 by the teaching of Vera Volkova, a remarkable teacher (born in St Petersburg) who had training from Maria Romanova (Ulanova's mother) and Vaganova before leaving Russia, and gained further experience dancing with George Goncharov in Shanghai and teaching in London. Volkova's classes in Russian style did not replace the Bournonville classes: they complemented them and helped the dancers to cope with ballets of the international repertoire.

France

PARIS OPERA BALLET

The ballet company of the Paris Opéra is the oldest surviving state ballet company: its origins can be traced back to the establishment by Louis XIV of the Académie Royale de Musique in 1671, before the separation of ballet and opera. Paris by then had become the most important centre of classical dancing, and the great French school flowered at the Opéra during the following century. Most of the great choreographers of the eighteenth century were French, and, although they found much greater scope in other countries than at the Opéra, they revived many of their finest works there; unfortunately none survived for long in the repertoire. During the heyday of the romantic ballet, in the middle years of the nineteenth century, the Paris Opéra was at the centre of things, and it was there that 'La Sylphide' and 'Giselle' were created. The boom subsided almost as quickly as it had arisen, and no great stars emerged to take the places of the five great international ballerinas, Taglioni, Grisi, Grahn, Cerrito and Elssler. In the next few decades the art of ballet decayed, in Paris as elsewhere, and all the great ballets which had been staged at the Opéra were lost. There was a short-lived flare of creative activity in 1870, when Arthur Saint-Léon staged 'Coppélia', with music by Delibes, a libretto of some merit, and a series of sparkling and witty performances as Swanhilda by the great French dancer Léontine Beaugrand. By this time ballet had degenerated to such an extent in Paris that male dancing had almost ceased, and the part of the hero Franz was taken, as was the custom of the day, by a danseuse *en travesti*. Poor Beaugrand received no other roles worthy of her talents, and there were no more great French dancers for several generations. In fact it became the fashion

always to have an Italian ballerina as the star of the Opéra, and the decadent French school was replaced at the Opéra by the Italian school: this was advanced technically but lacked the poetry and grace of the old French school. The Opéra in fact provided a sentimental and pretty entertainment for men-about-town who had dancers as mistresses and came to see them on stage.

When the Diaghilev company began to appear in Paris from 1909 onwards, the contrast between its masterpieces and the sentimental trivialities on display once a week at the Opéra was overwhelming: the Opéra improved a good deal, however, under the leadership of Jacques Rouché, who brought in Bakst and other fine designers, commissioned a production of 'Daphnis and Chloë' from Fokine, and above all brought in the great Russian ballerina Olga Spessivtseva as première danseuse étoile: when Spessivtseva finally appeared in 'Giselle' (restored to the repertoire in 1932), the impact was prodigious.

The Opéra gained in prestige also with the appointment of the young Diaghilev dancer and choreographer Serge Lifar as premier danseur and choreographer in 1930: Lifar soon dominated the Opéra completely, imposing his own brand of crude and unmusical, but theatrically effective, ballets.

No less significant was the arrival in Paris of a number of outstanding Russian teachers (notably Preobajenska) who made Paris a major centre of the Russian school. The teaching at the Opéra school remained much as before, but the most intelligent and ambitious of the dancers realised the importance of these teachers and began to study with them. Of these, Yvette Chauviré was the pioneer and by far the greatest: she worked hard with Boris Kniaseff, and developed into the

Opposite Josette Amiel and Jean-Pierre Bonnefous of the Paris Opéra in rehearsal.

Left Claire Sombert of the ballet company of the Paris Opéra.

first great French ballerina since Beaugrand; she was promoted to étoile in 1941, and danced the leading roles in the classics as well as starring in Lifar's ballets. Her influence on French dancing was enormous: stimulated by her remarkable artistry, other dancers studied with Rusian teachers, and the standard of dancing among the best Opéra soloists went up considerably in the following years.

Because of Lifar's strong personality and long domination of the Opéra (right up to 1958), his influence on French ballet was profound and lasting. It affected even those choreographers like Roland Petit and Maurice Béjart who rebelled against his ideas and style and set up companies of their own.

ROLAND PETIT

Roland Petit's position in ballet history is secure: he was the first French choreographer to create ballets of any real interest in France for nearly seventy-five years—in fact since Arthur Saint-Léon staged 'Coppélia' at the Opéra in 1870.

Petit was trained at the Opéra school, and showed such talent that he entered the company at the early age of fifteen in 1939. He had a strong drive towards choreography, but found no outlet for his ideas at the Opéra under Lifar, so he began to give recitals with Janine Charrat during the War. Immediately after the liberation of Paris, in the exciting atmosphere of the time, he found the stuffy climate within the Opéra insufferable and took part, with Boris Kokhno, in the establishment of the Ballets des Champs-Elysées, of which

he was chief choreographer, ballet-master and principal dancer. For this company he composed a number of lightweight but charming, fluent, entertaining and witty ballets, which contrasted in the most delightful and chic way with the pretentious and long-winded heaviness of the Lifar ballets. Typical of these ballets was 'Les Forains', which took the form of a series of divertissements presented by strolling players.

But Petit was unhappy in this company; he felt confined within projects in which choreography was less important than decor and gimmickry, and in 1948 he established his own company, the Ballets de Paris—the first of many such Petit companies. For this company he composed two of his most successful ballets, 'Les Demoiselles de la Nuit' and

'Carmen', and here he established his
own choreographic style.

'Carmen' was outstanding for the
fine opportunities it gave to Zizi Jeanmaire, Petit's future wife. In the title
role, Jeanmaire made a stronger impact
than any French dancer since Chauviré.
In many ways her career was like
Chauviré's: she too began as a *petit rat*
(student at the Opéra school), then
developed a superb classical style through
her studies with the Russian teacher
Boris Kniaseff, and then, working with
Roland Petit in roles created for her,
she developed a fascinating personality–
witty, elegant, seductive, assured and
intensely French. She was especially
good in the bedroom scene: though
Petit's erotic symbolism was rather crude
and obvious, Jeanmaire danced her role
with such purity of line, musicality

and spontaneity that she transformed
the movements almost into poetry.

In the next few years Petit devoted
himself to totally ephemeral works in
a music-hall style, and seemed to have
lost his way. But in 'Le Loup' (1953),
using another fairy-tale libretto by
Anouilh, he created for himself a touch-
ing role which suited his personality very
well: that of the wolf-man who is a
ferocious outsider, and yet is somehow
romantic and sympathetic. In later years
he devoted much of his efforts to large-
scale works like 'Cyrano de Bergerac'
and 'Notre Dame de Paris', in which
flashes of his real talent appeared amidst
long stretches of routine spectacle; and
also a very gimmicky ballet, 'Paradise
Lost' (1967), which he created as a
show-piece for Margot. Fonteyn and
Rudolf Nureyev, first for the Opéra,

and then for the Royal Ballet.

But his real talent re-emerged very
clearly in 'Les Chants de Maldoror',
based on the famous work of that name
by Lautréamont, in which he found
themes (obsession, panic and monsters)
which were admirably suited to his
special talents, calling from him his own
highly sophisticated blend of twisted,
cruel eroticism and 'camp' theatricalism.
Like 'Carmen', this ballet came to a very
effective climax in an erotic pas de deux:
in this case with a girl-spider (wonderfully danced by Danièle Jossi) taking
possession of a desperate man (Petit
himself). This was some of the best
choreography Petit had ever done: inventive, disturbing, cruel and voluptuous.

*Opposite John Cranko's 'The Prince of
the Pagodas' with Paul Vondrak as the
Prince and Suzanne Kirnbauer as
Belle Rose.
(Ballet company of Vienna Staatsoper).*

*Below Kathleen Gorham in Rudolf
Nureyev's production of 'Raymonda' for
the Australian Ballet.*

The Dispersion

INTRODUCTION

In the early stages of ballet, when it formed one part of court entertainments bringing together singing, dancing and spectacular scenic display, the leading dancers, teachers and choreographers were Italian. They were much in demand at this time outside Italy, and Italian was the international language of ballet. Then, from the seventeenth century to the end of the third quarter of the nineteenth century, ballet was dominated by French dancers, teachers and choreographers; they worked all over Europe, and the language of ballet was French. There was a period towards the end of the nineteenth century when Italian star dancers carried all before them in France, Russia and elsewhere; but this phase did not last long. For soon Russia emerged as the new leading country in ballet; Russian dancers, teachers and choreographers settled all over the world, and during most of the first half of this century the language of ballet was Russian. With the rapid development of ballet in Britain, and of ballet and its offshoot modern dance in the United States, these two countries began in their turn to export dancers, teachers, choreographers and artistic directors over much of the world; after the Second World War the language of ballet in a great many countries became English – though meanwhile Russian became the ballet language in the new Communist countries, and Belgian ballet under Béjart continued to speak French.

AUSTRALIA

Australians have a great talent for ballet, and this country has produced fine dancers ever since ballet training began there in the thirties. The most ambitious of these dancers came to Britain to make a career, the trail blazed by Helpmann being followed by Elaine Fifield, Lucette Aldous, Kathleen Gorham and many others. Performances of ballet were established in Australia with great success on the Ballet-Russe pattern by Edouard Borovansky, a Czechoslovakian dancer who had had extensive experience with the de Basil Ballet-Russe company from 1932 to 1939, and stayed behind after a visit to Australia by this company in 1939. He established his own school in 1940, and the Borovansky Company in 1941, with a typical Ballet-Russe repertoire. Booked by the powerful theatrical firm J. C. Williamson Theatres, the company played for astonishingly long seasons in the small number of big cities where the population of Australia is concentrated: though Borovansky had to dissolve the company from time to time, he did a great deal to establish a strong tradition of ballet in Australia before his untimely death in 1959.

In 1962 the Australian Ballet was set up by the directors of the Australian Elizabethan Theatre Trust and J. C. Williamson Theatres, and they engaged Peggy van Praagh as artistic director. Peggy van Praagh had been Tudor's leading danseuse in England, creating major roles in all his ballets, and she ran his company for a time after his departure for the United States in 1939, She then danced for the Sadler's Wells Ballet, and was ballet mistress of the Sadler's Wells Theatre Ballet. She took over the Borovansky company for a year after his death, and so was the obvious choice to direct the Australian Ballet (which used most of the Borovansky dancers).

The repertoire of the new company followed closely on the lines of that of the Royal Ballet, a repertoire with which Peggy van Praagh was very familiar: 'Swan Lake', 'Coppélia', 'Les Rendezvous' (the first ballet created by Ashton for the Vic-Wells Ballet). There was also a ballet with an Australian theme, 'Melbourne Cup', with choreography by Rex Reid, an Australian dancer trained at the Sadler's Wells School who had danced with two English companies and a Ballet-Russe company before returning to Australia. It was easy to see the origins of Rex Reid's light-entertainment style in various Massine ballets, in Ashton's 'Les Patineurs' and in Roland Petit's music-hall ballets; but Rex Reid had ideas of his own, such as using five dancers to represent the horses, and presenting them as if they were fairies in 'The Sleeping Beauty'. Moreover, the ballet

Below Rex Reid's 'Melbourne Cup'; the
brawl scene (Australian Ballet).

Opposite Peggy van Praagh, co-director of
the Australian Ballet. In the thirties, in
London, she was Antony Tudor's leading
female soloist.

was graced by some very witty décor and costumes in Victorian style by Ann Church, with much of the charm of Constantin Guys: this was highly sophisticated designing, and not in the least provincial.

When the company appeared in London in 1965, as part of the Commonwealth Arts Festival, it was only three years old; but it looked admirably assured, with a number of soloists who had previously had wide experience, in the Borovansky company, various European companies, or in both. It had an admirable prima ballerina in Kathleen Gorham, who had had experience as soloist in the Ballet Rambert, the Sadler's Wells Theatre Ballet, the Cuevas company, the Borovansky company and so on. At this time the company commissioned a production of 'Raymonda' from Nureyev, and staged two new ballets by Helpmann, an Australian who joined Peggy van Praagh as co-director – a very familiar pattern in the development of national ballet. In some respects Helpmann's ballet 'Yūgen' showed the company at its best – with superb costumes and décor by Desmond Heeley, inspired by Japanese principles but without copying the décor of Noh or Kabuki, and admirable performances by Kathleen Gorham and Garth Welch in the principal roles; but Helpmann's attempts at going Japanese were very superficial, being quite unsuited to his traditional theme (that of the great Noh play 'Hagoromo'); he mixed together ballet, folk dance and tricks with fans in a way suited only to light entertainment, of the type provided by the Japanese music-hall troupes.

GERMANY

Introduction

One of the most intriguing features of cultural life in Germany since the Second World War has been the tremendous rise in interest in classical ballet; in fact ballet has almost completely replaced modern dance, which in the twenties and early thirties had, together with a fusion of modern dance and ballet, as in the work of Kurt Jooss, taken over almost completely from ballet. In the aftermath of the First World War, those living in a defeated and conflict-ridden Germany were strongly drawn towards expressionism in all the arts, and this gave a great impetus to the rise of expressionist modern dance. Under the Nazis, modern dance was at first tolerated, in spite of its expressionism, because it was, or at least seemed to be, a purely German invention: it was only some years later that it was brought under strict Nazi control, and, like all the arts in Nazi Germany, lost its creative spark. After the Second World War the Germans swung just as violently against modern dance as they had swung towards it after the first. Modern dance was associated in people's minds with a discredited past which everyone wanted to forget, while ballet offered a serenity and orderliness in violent contrast to the chaos all about, the physical and the spiritual ruins; it also opened doors to the rest of the world, helping the Germans to break out of the isolation forced on them by the Nazis, and reinforced by the War.

This created a great demand for ballet in post-war Germany; at first this had to be satisfied by visiting companies, for Germany lacked classically trained dancers, teachers and choreographers, and so the Intendants of the various opera houses set out to fill the demand by building up ballet companies with the aid of dancers, teachers and choreographers from abroad. Results were very erratic, because of the way ballet is staged in Germany. It differs very much from that in other countries, mainly because the history of Germany has brought about great decentralization in the performing arts. The country was not unified until much later than the other great states of Europe – not, in fact, until 1871; in the dozens of small princedoms, dukedoms and kingdoms, each ruler had had his court and (quite often) his court theatre, with companies of actors, singers and dancers. These theatres and their companies were preserved by the authorities of the cities and constituent states of the German Empire and the Federal Republic: in fact, it was taken for granted that each city of any size should have its civic or state theatre, and provide theatrical entertainment for the citizens along with other services such as street lighting, police, public libraries and so on. Moreover there was (and is) healthy rivalry between those financing and controlling the various theatres, and subsidies are relatively high.

Because of this cultural heritage, the Bundesrepublik (West Germany) now has about fifty-five ballet companies in its various opera houses, and there is a corresponding profusion of companies in the rather smaller German Democratic Republic (East Germany). This would seem to represent an enormous quantity of ballet, and because of the decentralization one would expect great diversity. In fact ballet has low status within most German opera houses; the standard is usually appallingly bad, and there is comparatively little variety. The Intendants, knowing very little about ballet outside Germany and not appreciating the nature of choreography, tend to administer ballet in such a way that high standards are impossible. No repertoire is maintained: each year, apart from staging the dances in the operas, the resident ballet-master is expected to stage a small number of ballet programmes, each of which is given a small number of performances (just enough for all sub-scribers to see each programme once); and even when ballets of the international repertoire are staged, the local ballet-master is expected to provide his own choreography; in fact, choreography is treated as something quite ephemeral, the equivalent of the production of a play or opera. Lacking good teachers and choreography, dancing often in operas but seldom in *Balletabenden* (ballet evenings – programmes consisting exclusively of ballet), the dancers have no chance to reach high standards.

Fortunately there are a few German opera houses where the Intendants have realized that to bring ballet up to a reasonable standard they must administer it in a very different way, and in these companies (in Stuttgart, Hamburg, Berlin, Munich and a few other cities) German ballet has improved enormously.

Stuttgart

The ballet company of the Württembergisches Staatsoper in Stuttgart has an important place in ballet history: it was here that in 1760-7 the great Noverre, lavishly subsidized by Duke Karl Eugen, who had a passion for opera and ballet, created some of his finest works. No traditions of ballet have been preserved from that period, but ballet in Stuttgart shared in the general upsurge of German ballet after the Second World War, and the standard of dancing reached in the early fifties was very creditable, being well above the usual German standard. It was given a further stimulus by the employment of Nicholas Beriosoff as director of the ballet company in the latter half of the fifties.

The improvement in quality of this company in the sixties was so impressive that Germans began talking about it as the 'German ballet-miracle': this development was due to the vision of the Intendant, Walter Erich Schäfer, who brought in John Cranko and backed him

*Below John Cranko and Lynn Seymour
talking to Elphine Allen at a time when
she was one of the Royal Ballet's
choreologists. Later she became
choreologist to the Australian Ballet.*

in a series of reforms which adapted this company to the real requirements of ballet.

One of Cranko's most important reforms was to bring in quite a number of fine soloists from abroad – notably the elegant Marcia Haydée from Brazil, and others from the United States and Britain. He also reorganized the training in the classes, bringing in the English teacher Anne Woolliams.

No less important was his establishment of something revolutionary in Germany: a repertoire, performed from season to season, instead of a number of works staged for one season and then scrapped. With the rising standard of performance, the audience flocked to see the ballet, and this made it possible for Cranko and the Intendant to increase the number of performances to a level unheard of in Germany. (This was possible because the Staatsoper had two theatres at its disposal.) In 1969 the ballet company became quite independent of the opera company, another revolutionary innovation.

Cranko's achievements as a choreographer in London showed only a limited talent, but he now had a chance to create far more freely than in England, and by the standards prevalent in Germany before his arrival, his ballets were a major step forward. Moreover he commissioned ballets from others – notably 'Las Hermanas', a ballet based on a play by Lorca which he commissioned from Kenneth MacMillan – and staged ballets from the international repertoire.

Conditions within the Stuttgart company were in fact quite comparable with those in big companies outside Germany, and the company dancers, both German and imported, responded well. In fact Cranko and his associates established very clearly that a German ballet company could reach international standards, and this opened up a brighter future for the whole of German ballet.

The extraordinary impact that Cranko made in Germany can be judged from the fact that in 1968 he was appointed chief choreographer of the Bayerische Staatsoper in Munich while continuing to direct the Stuttgart company.

AUSTRIA

Austria is now a small country, but its capital is one of the world's greatest cities. Ancient, cosmopolitan Vienna, bringing together German, Italian and Slav cultural traditions in its own unique synthesis, was for centuries the capital of a great empire, and Viennese ballet has a long and rich history. Unfortunately only one of the ballets staged in Vienna in the eighteenth and nineteenth centuries survives: 'Die Puppenfee', a fairy-tale entertainment about dolls coming to life, staged by Josef Hassreiter in 1888.

The court of the imperial Hapsburgs naturally had its opera and ballet, and in fact baroque spectacles in Vienna in the seventeenth century rivalled those at Versailles; but the greatest period of Viennese ballet came in the latter part of the eighteenth century. At a crucial period in the development of ballet as an independent art, Vienna became the centre of the ballet world, thanks to the vision and enterprise of the Intendant of the Imperial and Royal Court Opera, Count Durazzo. Like Diaghilev, Durazzo brought great artists together in a creative and far-sighted way: the composer Gluck, the librettist Calzabigi, the great choreographer Angiolini, and the supreme choreographer of the time, Noverre.

Ballet continued to flourish in Vienna until the middle of the nineteenth century, with a ballet company containing French, Italian and Austrian dancers, and ballets staged mainly by French choreographers. One of the five greatest ballerinas of the romantic ballet, Fanny Elssler, was Viennese, and Vienna was one of the cities where these ballerinas dazzled audiences in the standard romantic ballets of the day. However, Viennese ballet subsequently suffered the same decline as elsewhere.

Between the wars modern dance flourished in Austria much as it did in Germany; in fact one of the leading figures in the modern-dance world of Central Europe was an Austrian. This

Above Vaslav Orlikovsky talking to ballet mistress, Gerlinde Dill, at a rehearsal of the ballet company of the Vienna Staatsoper.

Opposite Erika Hanka's 'Medusa' with Christl Zimmerl (centre) as Medusa and Suzanne Kirnbauer (l) as one of Medusa's companions (Ballet company of the Vienna Staatsoper).

was Rosalia Chladek, who taught at the famous Hellerau-Laxenburg School from 1924, and was artistic director of the school and its company from 1930 to 1938.

After the War there was much the same swing from modern dance to ballet as there was in Germany, and the standard of dancing of the ballet company gradually improved after 1954, thanks to the appointment of Gordon Hamilton as teacher and ballet master. Born in Australia, Hamilton had been trained in Paris by Preobajenska and in London at the Rambert School, and became a leading dancer in the Sadler's Wells Theatre Ballet and Roland Petit's Ballets de Paris. When he joined the Vienna company its programmes were dominated by the works which Erika Hanka, the director of the company, had been creating for it since 1941. Of Austrian origin, Erika Hanka had worked as a dancer mainly in Germany and was greatly influenced by modern dance; her attempts at working in a more classical vein had much the same awkwardness as those of her German contemporaries in German opera houses at this time. Nevertheless she saw the importance of providing the company with an international repertoire including the major nineteenth century and modern classics, and staged with the proper choreography instead of with local choreography; and a renaissance in Viennese ballet began during her last years with the company. She died in 1958.

1955 was a crucial year for this revival, for in this year, as part of the festivities celebrating the reopening of the great Staatsoper (much damaged in the War), Gordon Hamilton staged a fine production of 'Giselle'. The re-establishment of a standard of ballet in keeping with the splendour of the theatre and of Viennese performances of opera and instrumental music was slowed down by Gordon Hamilton's death in 1959, and the

appointment as director of the ballet company of an expressionist choreographer with very little understanding of classical ballet, Aurel Milloss; but progress continued after 1966 with the appointment of Vaslav Orlikovsky as ballet-director and the staging of a variety of works from the international ballet repertoire – notably Orlikovsky's production of 'The Sleeping Beauty', three Balanchine ballets 'Apollo', 'Four Temperaments' and 'Serenade', a production by Harald Lander of his ballet 'Etudes', the Ninette de Valois ballet 'Checkmate', and productions of 'Swan Lake' and 'Don Quixote' by Nureyev. Moreover, some of the finest (and most expensive) of the international stars of the day were brought in as guest artists: Nureyev, Fonteyn, Beriosova and others.

But – something of crucial importance artistically – the company was now producing its own stars of international stature. Some years earlier Willi Dirtl had emerged as a male character dancer of fire and dynamism, and now Karl Musil stood out in the company as something extremely rare: a tall, handsome classical danseur with temperament, style and noble elegance, as well as a strong technique, excellent line and impressive dramatic ability; he had some Czech blood, and was in some ways rather Slav, but he was in fact cosmopolitan in a very Viennese way, and would have fitted admirably into any great ballet company. (He had a sensational success partnering Beriosova with the Royal Ballet in London, inspiring her to dance with unaccustomed passionate intensity.) Another remarkable artist to go to the top in Vienna in the second half of the sixties was Suzanne Kirnbauer: her strong attack, clean line, powerful temperament and very individual style enabled her to dominate the stage whenever she appeared, even in an abstract ballet like 'The Four Temperaments', which gave

little scope for her dramatic gifts.

By this time the Staatsoper ballet had gone a long way towards re-establishing standards of production and performance worthy of its great old traditions. It had a number of things in its favour – notably lavish subsidies, the keen interest in ballet in Vienna (this city now supported no less than three permanent companies), a number of young home-grown stars of international stature, and an international repertoire with authentic choreography. In fact it had broken clean away from many of the crippling features of the Central European opera-ballet tradi-tion; to make further progress it needed to break away from certain other hindrances. One was limitation to a quite inadequate number of performances each month; another was isolation from the work of the creative artists who were shaping the development of world ballet in the second half of the twentieth century, rather as Calzabigi, Angiolini, Noverre and Gluck shaped ballet in the second half of the eighteenth century.

Right George Balanchine's 'Four Temperaments' with Suzanne Kirnbauer (Ballet company of the Vienna Staatsoper).

Opposite and next page Maurice Béjart's version of 'The Rite of Spring' (Ballet of the 20th Century).

BELGIUM & MAURICE BEJART

There are a number of ballet companies associated with opera houses in Belgium, notably in Antwerp and Liège, but the one associated with the Théâtre Royal de la Monnaie in Brussels is totally different from any other opera-house ballet, in Belgium or anywhere. It is completely the creation of one man, Maurice Béjart, and expresses his outlook and aesthetic in every detail.

Béjart was born in Marseilles, and from an early age showed a passion for the theatre, dreaming of becoming a producer of plays. He was trained at the ballet school of the Marseilles Opera and danced there until 1945. In 1947-9 he was a member of the Roland Petit company, and was much influenced by this experience; he also danced in Swedish and English companies. In 1953 he organized his first company, the Ballets de l'Etoile, to perform his ballets at the Theatre de l'Etoile in Paris.

In 1959 he received from Maurice Huisman, the recently appointed and very enterprising director of the Théâtre Royal de la Monnaie, an invitation which was to prove as crucial in his career as the one received by Ninette de Valois from Lilian Baylis in 1931, or that received by Balanchine and Kirstein in 1949 from Morton Baum. Huisman was determined to completely reorganize the dreary ballet company of the Monnaie, and had already invited in the Western Theatre Ballet from England and the Janine Charrat company from France. He now invited Béjart to bring his company to the Monnaie and to stage with it and the other groups a new production of 'The Rite of Spring'. This had such success that Huisman made Béjart ballet director of the Monnaie, with his own company, now called the Ballet of the Twentieth Century.

In 'The Rite of Spring' Béjart found music and a theme, or rather the possibility of imposing a theme, which suited him perfectly, and in this work his talent was seen at its best. The original story was largely ignored: he made the ballet into the most crude and earthy expression of primitive eroticism. The movements were simple and repetitive, and linked to the music in a very obvious way; the whole work hurled itself at the spectator with the violence characteristic of early expressionism. In more than one sense this version of the ballet was atavistic: in its style and aesthetic it went back to the modern dance of the early twenties in Germany and Russia. Béjart has continued to work mainly in this expressionist way, though no theme has suited his talent quite as perfectly as the one he imposed on 'The Rite of Spring'.

One of the strangest aspects of Béjart's artistic personality is that he thinks like a modern dancer, and keeps edging towards modern dance in his choreography, but he uses classically trained dancers, and shows no concern with the highly developed modern-dance techniques of modern America. He is not much concerned with choreography in the usual sense of the word: he is concerned, rather, to create the most striking possible theatrical effects, and uses the most direct and obvious, even banal, means to achieve these effects.

Another paradoxical aspect of a very paradoxical artist is his concern to staff his highly cosmopolitan company with dancers who not only have strong classical techniques, but are good-looking as well. The girls are ravishing, and the men strikingly handsome in face and body. This concern for beauty was in strange opposition to the crudity, ugliness and violence that, for years, characterized much of his choreography.

In the late sixties, however, he began to compose works such as 'Romeo and Juliet', 'Neither Flowers nor Crowns', inspired by Petipa, and 'Bakhti', inspired by Hinduism, with Indian sitar music, which were less crudely expressionist.

With his flair for publicity, and his talent for staging huge mixed-media spectacles in circuses and arenas as well more conventional works in theatres, Béjart has given ballet a new image. When he staged Beethoven's Ninth Symphony at the Royal Circus as an abstract-symbolic symphonic ballet, taking up the ideas started by Lavrovsky in 1924 and further developed by Massine in the thirties, this production was seen by no less than 100,000 people – one-tenth of the population of Brussels. In other huge auditoriums, in Avignon, Paris and elsewhere, he has attracted comparable audiences, bringing in people who would never normally go to ballet. For Béjart it is the general effect which matters, not the detail of choreography.

THE NETHERLANDS

Above and opposite Glen Tetley's 'Mythical Hunters' as revived for Nederlands Dans Theater.

In the early decades of the twentieth century there was almost no theatrical dancing of any kind in the Netherlands, and nothing to suggest that in the second half of the century that country would become one of the world centres of ballet.

It was a German dancer, Gertrud Leistikow, who reintroduced theatrical dancing into the Netherlands: she founded modern-dance schools in the four biggest cities in the early twenties, and the dancers emerging from these schools began to give recitals, just as in Germany. But there was a profound reaction against everything German after the Second World War; the swing away from German modern dance was even more powerful than in Germany, and there was a corresponding rise in interest in classical ballet.

The first ballet company to be established after the War was Scapino, which was established to give performances for children. It was founded by Mrs Hans Snoek in 1945, and has flourished ever since under her direction.

In 1947 the Ballet der Lage Lander was formed, with Mascha Ter Weeme as artistic director. English dancers, teachers and choreographers contributed a great deal to the development of this company.

A third company, the Nederlands Ballet, was established in 1958 by Sonia Gaskell. Born in Kiev, she began working as teacher and ballet-mistress in Paris in 1936, and in 1939 moved to the Netherlands, also to teach ballet. After the War she spent some years staging small-scale experimental works with a small group before establishing the fairly large Nederlands Ballet. She engaged as ballet-master and temporary director of her company the distinguished American teacher, ballet-master and choreographer Benjamin Harkarvy, who had just finished a year as director, choreographer and ballet-master of the

Royal Winnipeg Ballet.

There was still another company, the Opera Ballet of the Amsterdam Opera, directed in Lifarian style by the French dancer and choreographer Françoise Adret. In fact by 1958 the Netherlands had no less than four companies, with an astonishing quantity and diversity of ballet for so small a country.

In 1959 the Dutch Government began to favour the idea of combining the various subsidized companies together. In that year the Ballet der Lage Lander was combined with the Opera Ballet, and two years later this combined company was joined with the Nederlands Ballet to form the enormous National Ballet, under the direction of Sonia Gaskell.

This policy of fusion may have looked on paper like consolidation, but it could easily have led to the crushing of the diversity and vitality so characteristic of Dutch ballet. Fortunately this did not happen because of the enterprise of a small group of solo dancers in the Nederlands Ballet composed of the most mature and experienced of Dutch dancers. Led by Aart Verstegen, they broke away to set up the Nederlands Dans Theater, a company of a new type, containing soloists only, under the artistic direction of Benjamin Harkarvy, with the remarkable Carel Birnie as business manager and the outstanding Dutch dancers Willy de la Bye and Jaap Flier. In a sense this was a collective effort, offering great scope to all the dancers, and they showed from the start a marvellous spontaneity and individuality.

They also showed a precision and polish hitherto unknown in Dutch ballet. Benjamin Harkarvy worked extremely hard with them, in class and in rehearsal, and they responded magnificently.

The company settled into a pattern of work characteristic of Dutch ballet and well suited to the unique conditions in this small country. It gave about 160 performances a year, almost each of these a single performance in one of the admirable civic theatres which are so common in the Netherlands; every town of any size has one. For each performance the dancers usually travelled by coach during the afternoon to the town or city where they were to play, returning home to The Hague by coach after the performance. During the day they worked extremely hard on the preparation of an almost incredible number of new ballets: twelve or more a year. Dedicated to creative activity, the company made a point of showing something new at every town they visited.

One of the most important ways in which Harkarvy built up the company was by commissioning major works from leading American modern-dance choreographers: though Harkarvy himself was a classicist, demanding the highest classical purity of line, he also had a keen appreciation of the works of a choreographer like Anna Sokolow, and in fact commissioned from her two of her best works, 'Opus 58' and 'Rooms'. The fine Dutch solo dancers, though trained purely in classical ballet, took amazingly well to Anna Sokolow's tense barefoot patterns; and they were able eventually to do them *better* than the original New York cast, for they were able to mature their interpretations for month after month.

The company developed a widely varied repertoire, with neo-classical ballets by Harkarvy, stark modern-dance ballets by Anna Sokolow, jazz-dance ballets by the Dutch choreographer Hans van Manen, and many other types of ballet. Under these admirable conditions the dancers developed at great speed, and the company established itself as one of the finest in the world.

There were many changes in the years that followed. The Dutch choreographer

Hans van Manen became artistic director, in association with Benjamin Harkarvy, and created a series of ballets for the company. Some remarkable young dancers matured under Harkarvy's careful teaching and coaching—notably Alexandra Radius and Han Ebbelaar. The fine classical ballerina Marian Sarstädt joined the company, and showed herself just as gifted in modern dance as in classicism. The American dancer, Charles Czarny, forced to give up dancing because of knee trouble, became the company's modern-dance teacher, and developed a splendid form of modern-dance teaching well suited to its needs. A series of remarkable ballets was commissioned from Glen Tetley, including 'Pierrot Lunaire': here Käthy Gosschalk showed herself to have a marvellous capacity for powerful, seductive and witty dancing in the role of Columbine, as striking in her own way as Christopher Bruce was as Pierrot in the Rambert version. Another very successful Tetley production was 'Mythical Hunters', a mysterious work that was both primitive and sophisticated, showing tough, violent men as hunters and women as prey; it united mythology and contemporary symbolism with extraordinary power, and was staged with very poetic lighting. In 1969 Tetley joined the company as joint artistic director, replacing Harkarvy, who joined the Harkness Ballet; Tetley brought with him the fine American dancer Scott Douglas.

Meanwhile the National Ballet, with headquarters in Amsterdam, was developing in a rather different way. It had an enormous repertoire, covering every type of ballet; Sonia Gaskell kept adding new ballets, casting her net very wide, to establish a repertoire unique in the world. It included the major nineteenth-century classics, including 'La Sylphide', all the great Fokine ballets, charac-

Above Rudi van Dantzig, chief choreographer and co-director of the National Ballet of the Netherlands, on the stage of the Stadtschouwburg, Amsterdam, talking to Fernau Hall.

Opposite Rudi van Dantzig's 'Moments' (National Ballet of the Netherlands).

teristic works by such well-known choreographers as Massine, Dolin, Lander, Lichine, Taras, Carter, Lifar, Balanchine, Skibine, Béjart and Herbert Ross, and works by the American modern-dance choreographers Pearl Lang and Paul Taylor. It also included a number of works by Dutch choreographers, including a group of ballets by one of the most creative of young European choreographers, Rudi van Dantzig. The company included a number of remarkable principals, notably the splendid American Negro artist Sylvester Campbell – one of the finest classical male dancers in the world, noble and fiery; also the sensitive and mature Dutch male dancer Toer van Schaik, and such admirable Dutch danseuses as Tiny van Pel and Maria Koppers. Most of the dancers were Dutch, but the company included artists from a fine variety of countries.

Working with such dancers, the choreographers and producers were able to achieve splendid performances of each ballet when it was staged; unfortunately the company was not organized by Sonia Gaskell in such a way as to keep the ballets up to this standard, and they tended to lose quality after six months or so. In fact the task of maintaining in good order a repertoire of nearly a hundred ballets was beyond the ability of any ballet-master working in the traditional way; but a great step forward was taken in 1966 when the company took on the choreologist Wendy Vincent-Smith, trained in Benesh notation. She had the Herculean task of making choreographic scores of the ballets in the immense repertoire, and helping the ballet-masters to preserve and revive them in good shape.

The company's chief choreographer, Rudi van Dantzig, was trained in Sonia Gaskell's school and then danced in her various companies. Two powerful influences pushing him towards choreog-

raphy, and influencing his approach and style, were the neo-realist films of de Sica and a demonstration class by Martha Graham which he watched when she visited the Netherlands in 1954 with her company. He found his true path with 'The Family Circle' (1957), showing the development of the hero from childhood through adolescence, somewhat as Tudor did in 'Undertow'. Here he showed the beginnings of a remarkable gift for creating characters and suggesting emotional conflicts. In 'Jungle', choreographed for the National Ballet in 1961 to electronic music by Hank Bading, he created a striking picture of modern society as transposed into terms of jungle animals; in 'Monument for a Dead Boy', created for the Harkness Ballet and revived for the National Ballet, he treated a theme rather like that of 'The Family Circle' with much greater power, and in 'Moments', choreographed for the National Ballet, he interpreted the music of Webern in an abstract-classical way with subtle musicality and some remarkable groupings.

In 1968 Sonia Gaskell began to play a less active part in the administration of the company, sharing it with Rudi van Dantzig and the Belgian ballet-master and choreographer Robert Kaesen and soon they took over completely. In this way Rudi van Dantzig moved into a position of artistic leadership for which he was highly qualified, though still only thirty-five; it thus happened that at roughly the same time, in 1967-8, three gifted young men, Norman Morrice, Rudi van Dantzig and Lawrence Rhodes, became wholly or partly responsible for the artistic policy of three important companies.

Classical Dances of the East
INDIA

Introduction

The classical ballet of the West is old enough to seem venerable compared to modern dance; but it is a brash newcomer compared with the classical dances and dance-dramas of the East: in many Eastern countries the traditions go back nearly 2,000 years, and in India even further. Over these long centuries the dance styles as performed in temples and courts have developed great beauty of line and expression, and almost unimaginable variety: India alone has no less than eight distinct styles, each with its own highly specialized techniques of pure dance and dramatic expression; and in the many surrounding countries to which Indian styles have penetrated there are a great many other highly developed classical styles representing a fusion of Indian and local traditions.

In the early years of the twentieth century it seemed likely that the classical styles of India would die out. It was not generally realized that they were descended from the ancient and highly revered classical dance of India, and the surviving styles suffered from the loss of their traditional patrons, temples and princes.

But there were a few influential people who understood the great value of the classical styles, and fought for their rehabilitation. One by one the various styles were taken up by middle-class girls, who had training from traditional *gurus*, and the best of these became great artists rivalling the achievements of the traditional dancers. In fact there was a great renaissance in classical dancing after Independence, reflecting the pride of the Indians in their rich and ancient heritage; and though dancing by *devadasis*, temple dancers, almost ceased, the traditional dancers of styles not performed by *devadasis,* such as Kathak and Kathakali, shared in the renaissance, finding a new public to replace their traditional patrons.

There was now a new dispersion of Indian dancing to foreign countries. This began with far-ranging tours by companies based on Britain–notably those of the Uday Shankar company, based on Dartington Hall near Totnes, Devon, in the thirties and those of the London-based Ram Gopal company in the forties and fifties. In due course nearly all the Indian dancers and dance-companies began to move out from India and tour abroad.

At the same time Indians began to settle and to teach in foreign countries, while outsiders began to go to India for training and returned to teach in their own countries. This was specially true of the United States, where Indian dancing has been widely taught, and has had considerable influence on modern dance and jazz dance.

Ritha Devi

Each classical Indian style has it own outstanding exponents. In Kathak, for example, there is the great traditional danseuse Sitara Devi, the brilliant male dancer and choreographer Birju Maharaj, and a number of others; Bharata Natyam has Balasaraswati, the last of the great *devadasis,* a dancer who is unequalled in dramatic expression and devotional fervour, and there are magnificent Bharata Natyam dancers of later generations such as Yamini Krishnamurti. Kathakali dance-drama has its great traditional artists like Ramankutty and Shivashankar. Other styles too have their leading performers.

Ritha Devi stands out in two ways. One is her unparalleled versatility: she has mastered all eight of the classical styles, performs admirably in seven of them, with strict adherence to the techniques and special qualities of style and feeling of each, and is likely to include three or four styles in a single recital. Because these styles differ from each other in the most striking way, a solo recital by her has the impact of a

performance by a whole company, and on her world tours she has done much to spread an appreciation of Indian dance.

Her other great achievement is in showing to the full the magical sweetness, nobility, feminine lyricism, technical complexity, and dramatic intensity of Odissi, the style of Orissa State, which very nearly got lost with the decline in *devadasi* dancing, and has only recently become known outside Orissa. Ritha Devi has the beauty often found in women of the Tagore family, and when she stands in the 'thrice-bent' pose characteristic of Odissi she looks exactly like one of the dancers sculptured on the walls of ancient Orissa temples.

Her hands, telling a story, seem to take on a life of their own, and the moods they express are projected out to the audience by the most subtle and powerful facial expressions.

CEYLON & BALASUNDARI

One of the main streams of dispersion of Indian culture a millenium and more ago took the Buddhist religion and Indian dance, music, sculpture and architecture to Ceylon. Because of the closeness of Ceylon to India, the impact of Indian culture was profound and long-continued; and Ceylon today has a great classical form of male dancing, Kandyan, which is strikingly close in many ways to Kathakali, though the gestures are used in a purely abstract way.

In Ceylon temple danseuses used to perform the style now called Bharata Natyam in the shrines of Hindu gods within Buddhist temples; but this tradition was lost. In recent years a softened version of Kandyan has been widely taught to schoolgirls, but they could not hope to rival the great traditional male Kandyan dancers. Fortunately Bharata Natyam became re-established in Ceylon as one part of the new wave of dispersion which carried Indian dance to many countries after the Second World War.

The most important figure in this Ceylonese wave of dispersion was a beautiful young dancer called Balasundari. In her early teens she was sent to Madras on a Ceylon government scholarship to study at the great Bharata Natyam school of Kalakshetra, directed by Rukmini Devi (one of the most important pioneers in the rehabilitation of Bharata Natyam). Balasundari (whose ancestors had come to Ceylon from India centuries earlier) showed great talent for Bharata Natyam, and after long years of training she became a leading dancer in the Kalakshetra company. After leaving the company she toured widely in Europe, making a strong impact with her elegant strength of movement, purity of line, and crisp precise rhythms; she showed also a great

119

subtlety of feeling in dramatic expression.

In Ceylon, she continued her career as a dancer, and also started a school; her talent as a teacher was so remarkable that she soon had over a hundred pupils, and established Bharata Natyam in Ceylon as a major feminine classical style alongside the great masculine style of Kandyan.

Coming to live in London for a time, she soon established herself as an inspiring and meticulous teacher, and as a dancer with her own uniquely magical and delicate radiance.

THAILAND

Thailand is unique among the countries of South-East Asia in that it has never been a colony of a Western power; in its court dance-drama it has preserved with wonderful fidelity the ancient glories of a style very much influenced by Indian classical dancing and dance-drama. Thai dancing, like all the classical styles of South-East Asia, draws its themes from the Indian epics Ramayana and Mahabharata, and uses variants of Indian *mudras*, stylized hand-gestures, and head movements, as well as the characteristic Indian angularity of line, with turned-out hips and turned-up feet; the hands are trained to bend back from the wrist to an extraordinary extent, going far beyond anything in Indian dancing, and the dancers do not use the very fast, powerful and intricate foot-beats characteristic of most Indian classical dancing. The whole emphasis is on grace, elegance and poise, and no style is more elegant and aristocratic than Thai court dancing; it was never seen by the general public until the twenties of this century.

FLAMENCO DANCE OF SPAIN

Previous page Ritha Devi in 'Ahalya', one of the five solo dance-dramas at the heart of the Odissi repertoire. Ahalya bows in greeting to what she takes to be her husband, but is really Indra.

Previous page Balasundari in a Bharata Natyam solo: her pose represents Lord Siva in his cosmic dance creating, preserving and destroying the world.

Above and opposite Antonio in Flamenco solos.

Introduction

Strangely enough Spain has an ancient style of dance which is closely related to the classical Kathak dance of North India: there is hardly one technical feature of the Flamenco dance of Andalusia which does not have its exact equivalent in Kathak, and in fact the two styles must be regarded as cousins. The gypsies who have been performing Flamenco for centuries originated in India and still speak a language of Indian origin; but they did not bring Kathak with them in their wanderings. The Oriental style of dancing we now know as Flamenco reached Spain long before the gypsies; there may well have been Eastern influence on Spanish dance in Graeco-Roman times, and these influences became very strong during the many centuries (beginning with its conquest by Arabs in 711 AD) when Andalusia was one of the richest and most cultured parts of the great world of Islam, which stretched from Spain right across North Africa and the Middle East to North India and even beyond India to Java, Malaya and the Philippines.

Up to the twentieth century Flamenco was generally regarded in Spain as a vulgar sort of gypsy entertainment, and non-gypsies would never have dreamed of taking it up; it was largely thanks to the efforts of Manuel de Falla and Federico Garcia Lorca between the wars that people began to take seriously the gypsy styles of singing, guitar-playing and dancing, and to appreciate their antiquity and great artistic significance.

Antonio

The first non-gypsy to become a great Flamenco dancer was Antonio. Born in Seville, the largest city in Andalusia, he studied under the finest gypsy teachers, mastered every aspect of Flamenco, and became such a virtuoso that he established himself as one of the world's greatest dancers. At first he danced with his cousin Rosario as his partner, then appeared at the head of companies which he formed and rehearsed with painstaking attention to detail, showing a remarkable gift for choreographing suites of folk-dances so as to make the strongest impact in the theatre. He developed expertise in all forms of Spanish dance, and also in ballet, and he began to choreograph complete ballets in Spanish style. But he continued to give Flamenco great emphasis in his programmes, and showed imagination and fine organizing ability in staging the traditional improvised gypsy Cuadro Flamenco. Though, late in the sixties, his programmes became less well produced, he was still to be seen performing brilliantly in his favourite Flamenco solos.

Carmen Amaya

Gypsies revere the memory of Carmen Amaya (who died in 1963), for she ran an all-gypsy company with great success for many years, helping all her artists to give of their best, and herself dancing with exciting demoniacal power–what in Spanish is called *duende*.

When touring outside Spain and Latin America, she sometimes seemed to feel the need to win over audiences unused to the subtleties of Flamenco, and played up the popular image of the wild gypsy dancer: dancing every item as fast as possible, shaking her head so that her hair fell over her eyes, scowling ferociously, and concentrating on beating the stage with her feet with masculine violence. In reality she had a wide range as well as great virtuosity, and so was highly regarded by aficionados of Flamenco.

Her influence on other *bailaoras* has been profound, lasting and often regrettable. One sees a number of gypsy *bailaoras* who try to rival Carmen Amaya's immense impact by imitating the more superficial aspects of her art, but whose *duende* is distinctly phoney. This has contributed to a general trend towards neglect of the more subtle, ancient, noble and poetic aspects of Flamenco–a trend also to be observed thousands of miles away in Flamenco's cousin, the Kathak dance of North India. Fortunately both Flamenco and Kathak still have their great artists who preserve and do honour to the ancient traditions of their art.

National Dance Companies

MOISEYEV ENSEMBLE

One of the most striking developments in the dance world after the Second World War was the establishment all over the world of national companies, performing theatricalized versions of folk dances. Everywhere these companies have become the expression of national feeling, of pride in ancient and distinctive cultural traditions, and their formation is as natural a sequel to the achievement of independence as the setting up of an air-line.

The great pioneer of this development, most of which has taken place since the Second World War, is Igor Moiseyev: it was he who started the first of these national-dance companies in the Soviet Union in 1937, and it was he who first developed the methods needed to adapt national dances to the stage – the combination of elements from a number of traditional dances to give more variety, adaptation of the stage-patterns to look good from the front, and the building-up of the theatrical force of the steps with ballet technique while preserving the essential features and structures of the traditional style of each region.

Moiseyev is at heart a choreographer: he was trained at the Bolshoi Ballet School, began choreographing ballets for the Bolshoi for some years before he became involved with folk-dances, and established his own ballet company in 1967, while still continuing to run his great folk dance company. He is quite prepared to invent folk dances if neces-

BAYANIHAN PHILIPPINE DANCE COMPANY

LEBANESE DANCERS

sary – as he did for Byelorussian dancers, whose traditions had been lost – and often invents new steps in the manner of the dances of a region.

When Moiseyev first formed his company, his dancers were mainly amateur folk-dancers who had taken part in a folk dance festival; of thirty-five dancers, only a handful had had professional training, being, in fact, graduates of ballet schools. As a result of the enormous success of the company it grew larger and larger, eventually containing a total of 120 dancers; and so many other folk dance companies were formed in the Soviet Union that special schools were set up to train dancers for them, as well as the National Dance Department, headed by Moiseyev, of the Bolshoi School.

Right from the start Moiseyev showed himself a man of great versatility, and interested in every kind of folk dance. His very first programme included not only Russian and Ukrainian dances, but also those of the Caucasus (Georgia, Armenia, and Azerbaijan) and Soviet regions of Asia such as Kazakhstan; and he showed remarkable skill in catching the essential qualities of the more exotic dances and in teaching them to his dancers.

The company toured widely within the Soviet Union before and during the War, and since the War it has toured extensively outside the Soviet Union as well, doing much to inspire the creation of national companies everywhere. And everywhere Moiseyev has picked up local dances to add to his fantastic repertoire, making it by far the most varied folk dance company in the world.

Though Moiseyev is interested in all kinds of folk dances, his forte is the production for the stage of items involving speed, fire, power, gusto, brilliance and humour, and part of his achievement has been to develop a company of dancers able to produce all these qualities.

The Lebanon has been a busy crossroads for thousands of years, and Lebanese dances show many links with those of other countries, while at the same time preserving a characteristic gay buoyancy. The danseuses, with their fair skins, have a rather Parisian elegance and sophistication, while the men with their neat clipped moustaches and high black boots might almost be Caucasian.

The dances performed by this company are of two main types. Some are of the chain type, familiar in the Balkans under the name *kolo, hora,* and so on, but in fact found all over the Eastern Mediterranean: the dancers move in long lines, making neat little stamping movements, with the leader at the end of the line waving a knotted handkerchief, and the men sometimes doing rather more difficult steps with deep knee bends. The stage-patterns of the lines of dancers keep changing, and the general animation is helped by the rhythmic shouts of the dancers and beats of the drum. Chain dances are for both sexes together; the other main type of dance is confined to the girls, who sway their hips gently, changing weight from one foot to another, while making undulating movements of hands and arms.

The most exciting male item is a sword dance, with pairs of men clashing swords on each other's bucklers in a way which shows close affinity with the sword dances of Turkey and India.

One of the joys of the performances of this company is the sweet singing of Feirouz, an artist of exceptional charm, who is deservedly famous in the Arab world.

The Philippine Islands lie on the fringe of a number of different cultural regions, Indo-Malayan, Polynesian, and Japanese, and have been subjected to a great variety of cultural influences by conquerors, notably Arabian and Spanish. The result is that a great variety of dance-styles coexist in the various islands, and the superb Bayanihan company, the national company, does justice to all of them, thanks to many years of scholarly work by Helena Benitez and to the drive, intelligence and imagination of the company's director, Lucretia Reyes Urtuala.

The artists of this company are as good-looking, in their slender Malayo-Polynesian way, as the Georgians in theirs; they are all university students, for the company is run in conjunction with a university.

Of all the varied styles of the company, the most magical and fascinating are the very old ritual dances from mountain villages in North Luzon: the dancers move in complex patterns, or kneel in stylized, ritual immobility, and one can see links here with the most ancient ritual dances of Japan.

Other dances reflect Arabian influences, having typically Arabian sinuous arm movements combined with elements of the female court dances of Java, including *gamelan* music.

The most famous and popular of Philippine dances is '*Tinikling*', in which dainty and elegant girls, while moving their arms slowly and gracefully, move their feet briskly and with extreme and necessary precision between bamboo poles knocked rhythmically together by men standing on either side; this has become the national Philippine dance par excellence.

Opposite Lebanese Dancers performing a women's group dance.

*Left Georgian State Dance Company
performing a group dance in which trios of
two men and one woman circle the stage.*

*Above Bayanihan Philippine Dance
Company. A dance showing a blend of
Arabian and Javanese influences.*

WEST AFRICA

NATIONAL DANCE COMPANY OF JAMAICA

In Africa dancing lies right at the heart of all cultural activity, just as it does in India: much of the finest African sculpture takes the form of dance-masks, the instrumental music and singing is heard at its best as part of a dance, and dancing plays an essential role in African religious rituals. Africans all over the continent have a passion for dancing, finding in it an expression of their deepest feelings and giving them vital contact with the ancient traditions of their tribes.

In West Africa concern with the dance is particularly intense, and some newly independent countries of what was once French West Africa, Senegal, Mali, Guinea, and also Sierra Leone, once part of the British Empire, have set up admirrable national companies as an expression of their pride in their ancient traditions; actually Senegal had a fine company, Les Ballets Africains, well before independence.

Each of these countries has its own varied traditions embodied in the repertoires of its company, and the dancers differ a fair amount in physique and temperament, but certain things are common to the dancing of the whole of this vast area. These are charm, spontaneity, exuberance, rhythmic vitality and a refreshingly innocent and frank eroticism, quite untainted by Christian guilt-ridden Puritanism. Unmarried girls are commonly bare-breasted, and shake their breasts with great abandon, as an essential and integral part of complex rhythmic patterns involving the whole body. The men strike the ground boldly with the feet, and make the most astonishing leaps with suppleness and ease. Ritual mask dances are striking.

Not content just to stage programmes of theatricalized versions of traditional dances, the various companies attempt to fit the dances into a framework of ballets with simple stories. Sometimes the story-telling is naive and long-winded, and distracts one's attention from the admirable dances, but at its best this technique is very promising for the future of African dance-drama.

The problem facing Rex Nettlefold and Eddy Thomas, the two dancer-choreographers who founded the Jamaican National Dance Company after Jamaica was granted its independence, was much the same as that which faced Amalia Hernandez in Mexico–that of bringing together the different strands in their country's cultural heritage. They came to grips with it in a somewhat similar way, taking a good deal from American modern dance. The two men complemented each other very well, Rex Nettlefold being an intellectual, a lecturer at the University of Jamaica, and Eddy Thomas a dancer with a good deal of experience in American modern dance.

They took Jamaica's African heritage very seriously, reviving what they could, notably some fine African cult-drumming, and also taking some interesting items from other islands with an Afro-Latin heritage. But their main effort went into the composition of ballets on Jamaican themes, such as 'The Legend of Lover's Leap', based on a Jamaican legend of two slaves who fell in love and defied the girl's master. These ballets had some fine scenes, and some excellent male dancing in modern-dance style from Eddy Thomas, Rex Nettlefold and Bertie Ross; but the girls were less impressive, and many of the scenes were ineffective.

Nevertheless these ballets represented the only possible way forward for the company, which could not hope to find in the West Indies sufficient folk-dance material to continue as a national-dance company of normal type. Its future lay in becoming something much more like a modern-dance company of the Alvin Ailey type, and developing a strong modern-dance technique. A number of its dancers went to New York to study with Martha Graham, and its season in Kingston in the summer of 1968, organized by Rex Nettlefold to celebrate the sixth anniversary of Jamaican independence, showed a marked improvement in the quality of dancing, as well as a new work in jazz-dance style, 'Bach, Brubeck and Company', commissioned from Neville Black, which did much to help the development of the company, now solely directed by Nettlefold.

Eddie Thomas in 'Kas Kas' (National Dance Theatre Company of Jamaica).

GEORGIAN STATE DANCE COMPANY

BALLET FOLKLORICO DE MEJICO

The Georgian State Dance Company is outstanding in a number of ways: in the good taste and imagination informing every detail, the high standard of the choreography, the extreme care for authenticity, and the vitality, enthusiasm and good looks of the dancers. The women have round faces of staggering beauty, and as they move across the stage with a characteristic smooth glide as if they were mounted on castors, with inward-turned, serene facial expressions, they all seem reincarnations of the legendary Queen Tamara. The men are lean and wasp-waisted, with sinews of steel and proud hawk-faces, moving with dangerous sleekness in their soft boots, which are as flexible as gloves, and permit them to dance *on point*. In fact they seem to belong to a totally different world from that of the women: their movements are angular instead of soft, and they rejoice in great leaps, in spinning on their knees, and in stabbing their *pointes* into the ground with splendidly virile grace. In characteristically Georgian fashion they look passionate, heroic, intensely proud and aristocratic. And never for a moment does any element of bad taste or vulgar showmanship, such as garish costumes, creep into the programme. During long centuries when the Georgians were ruled by outside powers they hung on to their national identity to a large extent by continuing to perform their ancient songs and dances, and this has helped to give them a wonderful feeling for the past which they bring to life in all its quality and subtlety. The finest of the old Georgian dances, like 'Simd', an Ossetian wedding dance, are strangely moving and magical, giving the impression of an ancient ritual. In some old Georgian dances there are clear links with Indian folk-dances, as in 'Eastern Dance', which is very like Indian Marwari dances, while in the solos of Nino Ramishvili one can see hand movements which might well be derived from the *mudras* of classical Indian dancing.

Much of the credit for the extraordin-

ary quality of this company's performances must go to Nino Ramishvili, who directs the company with her husband Iliko Sukhishvili. At the head of every great national-dance company one always finds a remarkably creative person, with a strong personality and great flair for the theatre as well as sensitivity to the nuances of the different national styles; and Nino Ramishvili is a magnificent example of such a dancer/choreographer/teacher/producer/organizer.

Danseuses of the Ballet Folklorico de Mejico performing a group dance showing Spanish influence.

Like nearly all great national-dance companies, the magnificent Ballet Folklorico de Mejico owes its success to the vision, drive and choreographic ability of one person: in this case that of its founder and director, Amalia Hernandez. She was trained in ballet and Spanish dance, and then underwent extensive training in Graham-style modern dance. Her dancers have regular modern-dance classes, and this helps them to give power, control and precision to their work.

Characteristic of Mexico is the combination of Amerindian and Spanish cultural elements, and fine examples of both coexist in the repertoire. In some dances there are groups of dancers performing in unison the fast stamping footwork of the solo, professional style of Andalusia (Flamenco), while the *Danza de La Moros*, very close in style to English Morris dances, represents the battle between Christians and Moors in Spain but actually goes back to much earlier times. But the most fascinating of all the items are the Indian dances: notably the ancient Aztec dances of the Quetzals, performed by men in huge Aztec feathered head-dresses, and the unforgettable and very moving Deer Dance of the Yaqui Indians. In this traditional dance a solo male dancer, moving with extraordinary grace, lightness and dramatic intensity, and carrying a rattle, imitates in a stylized choreographic way the movements of a wounded deer; the end of this dance, with the wounded deer stumbling to a halt, is as moving as a fine performance of the Fokine solo immortalized by Pavlova, 'The Dying Swan'.

Like Moiseyev, Amalia Hernandez is very much a choreographer, and has formed a ballet company; her abilities as choreographer are seen at their best in an item like 'Wedding on the Isthmus of Tehuantepec', which contains in symbolic form courtship, wedding and procreation; though the wedding is a Christian one, the rituals take one back to a very ancient pre-Christian era.

New Directions
INTRODUCTION

One would think that after so much experimental avant-garde choreography, nothing really new is possible. Yet new types of choreography are likely to emerge whenever choreographers work under new conditions, meeting new problems. Sometimes they fail to rise to the challenge, but sometimes they succeed: and, with the world changing so fast, fresh challenges keep on emerging, calling new kinds of choreography into existence.

NEW TRENDS IN MODERN DANCE OUTSIDE USA

Graham modern dance was brought to Britain very early on, by the Australian dancer and choreographer Margaret Barr. She went to study with Graham in 1928, and returned to Britain in 1930 to start a company of her own at Dartington Hall, Devon, where she enjoyed the support of Mr and Mrs Elmhirst, along with Uday Shankar. She differed considerably from Graham in temperament: she was above all interested in dance-drama and in fact called her company the Dance-Drama Group. She developed a technique and style of her own, reflecting her aesthetic ideals and also a social and artistic climate very different

from that of the United States. Her finest work was 'The Three Sisters', a powerful dance-drama using a good deal of mime in a very un-Grahamish way.

After disbanding her group in 1938, Margaret Barr returned to Australia, and it was a very long time before a modern-dance group comparable to the Dance-Drama Group was launched in Britain. It was not, in fact, until 1967, when the London Contemporary Dance Group was launched by Robin Howard at East Grinstead as a natural outgrowth of the London School of Contemporary Dance (providing training in Graham modern dance), which he had established the previous year.

The programme included a promising item, 'Witness of Innocence', by the young Canadian dancer David Earle. A later workshop programme organized by him included some interesting dances; 'Dark Voyage', by the Australian Barry Morland, was intriguing in that it had much the same theme as Margaret Barr's 'Three Sisters', but treated this in a more symbolic and ritualistic way.

In 1969 Robin Howard, showing great vision and courage, created an important centre for the performance of all kinds of dance: The Place, converted from a drill-hall. At last it was possible for the London Contemporary Dance Company, directed by the Graham dancer Robert Cohan, to give regular London seasons and stage a wide variety of new works, most of the choreographers drawing on Graham traditions, but some at times on other sources as well. Together with the work done by the Ballet Rambert, this brightened the prospect for the development of indigenous modern dance styles and techniques.

Comparable things are happening in other countries, such as Israel, Japan, Jamaica, Argentina and Canada. Creative modern dance is by no means as widespread as ballet, but this may come.

TELEVISION BALLET & JUAN CORELLI

The problems involved in presenting dancing on the small screen are so grave that one would imagine that it must always lack the impact of the real thing on a stage. In fact television dancing can make just as strong an impact as dancing on stage, if the choreography is composed for the screen and imaginative use is made of the full resources of the medium. The artist who has done more than anyone else to establish television ballet as an art-form in its own right, with its own laws and making its own characteristic effects, is Spanish-born Juan Corelli. He has created over fifty television ballets all over the world, using a wide variety of subjects and styles, and has established the great possibilities of this new form.

After being trained as a dancer in Barcelona, London and Paris he trained in Paris as a film editor, and from the moment he began to create ballets for television he worked not so much as a choreographer, in the usual sense of the word, but as a creator of images. Before starting work on a ballet, he planned every image on a story-board, and he worked out the choreography in the rehearsal room to produce exactly those images.

Each movement was devised to be seen by a particular camera at a particular angle, using a particular lens, and forming part of a sequence, with cuts from shot to shot carefully timed to match the movements of the dancer and the music. Close-ups, instead of breaking the flow of movement, were planned to form an integral part of the telechoreography.

In Paris in 1958, at the beginning of his career, Corelli was fortunate to win the support of a very enterprising French television producer of musical programmes, Lucienne Bernadac, and she gave him four ballets a year. For these he brought in leading dancers from many countries, and in each successive work he tackled his subject in a fresh way suited to the theme. In 'Jeux', for example—making a television version of the Nijinsky-Debussy *poème dansée*—he brought together Claire Motte from the Paris Opéra, Gisèle Deege from Berlin and Terry Gilbert from London and evolved a fluid televisual style, with constantly moving cameras, to reflect the impressionism of Debussy's music; for close-ups, the choreography provided for the dancer to move up to the camera.

Great dancers were delighted to work for him because they knew he would demand of them qualities never normally required by choreographers, and would use cameras to project these qualities powerfully to the audience.

There was Lucette Aldous and John Gilpin looking strikingly unlike their normal selves in the contemporary fantasy 'Etrange Nuit', which was without music in the usual sense of the word, but had instead natural sounds like footfalls: when there was music it was because the young man turned on the radio. In 'Le Ballet Cruel' Beriosova looked almost unrecognizable as a ferocious, voluptuous, black-haired beauty of the Belle Epoque.

While still working in Paris from time to time, Corelli began to work frequently in other countries, the Netherlands, East and West Germany, Belgium, Britain, Switzerland, Australia, the United States, Canada and so on. He began more and more to film his ballets rather than record them on video tape, finding this gave him much greater freedom in establishing the exact rhythms of cutting he needed for his effects and the exact interplay between movement and music. Corelli has profited from the introduction of colour television to achieve effects previously impossible, working closely with the designer on the planning of each shot. Alwin Nikolais, greatest of abstract modern-dance choreographers, has done magical things on colour television in the United States by subjecting the images of his dancers to complex electronic manipulation; and no less expertise and imagination has been shown by Norman McClaren, the great Canadian pioneer of animated films, in producing magical frieze-patterns from the movements of two classical dancers in a pas de deux. A time will come when choreography for the screen will equal and complement the finest achievements of stage choreography.

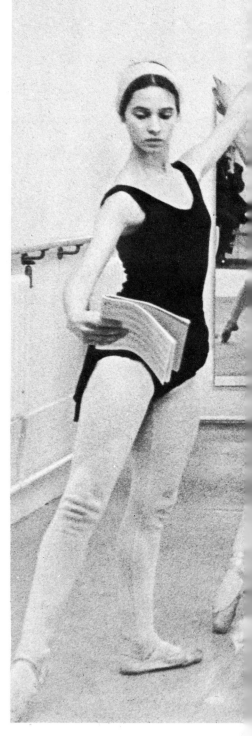

CHOREOLOGY

Previous page Students of the Royal Ballet Senior School having a class in Benesh Movement Notation.

Barry Morland's 'Dark Voyage', with Ruth Posner as one of the three sisters (London Contemporary Dance Theatre, 1968).

Opposite Part of the choreographic score in Benesh Notation of Glen Tetley's 'Ziggurat' made by the Ballet Rambert's choreologist Ann Whitley, with her reference sketches of tubular décor, moved by dancers, at the top.

The invention by Rudolf Benesh of a movement notation as precise, economic, fast and efficient as the alphabet and music notation made possible very important changes in the running of dance companies. First the Royal Ballet adopted it in 1955 for use in the company and school; later many other companies adopted it, in Britain and in various countries throughout the world. Companies deciding to use the notation took on to their staffs choreologists trained at the Institute of Choreology in London; these had the task of writing down each ballet or modern-dance work as it was staged and then using their movement scores to revive it at a later date as re-

quired. The saving in rehearsal time at revivals was of course enormous and now for the first time, it was possible to revive a work with the original choreography correct in every detail.

Just as Marie Rambert was called on by Diaghilev to tackle the score of 'The Rite of Spring' in 1913, the young choreologist Ann Whitley faced a great challenge, on joining the Ballet Rambert in 1967, when she found herself called on to work with Glen Tetley, notating 'Ziggurat' as he created it. Stockhausen's electronic music was fiendishly difficult, and she did not even have the 'graph' of the music to help her.

The movements she had to record were quite new, and Tetley, encouraging each dancer to do certain patterns in his own way, expected her to record every variation. He required her, moreover to notate the lighting and the movements of the scenery, since these formed an integral part of his choreography; also the changes in the projections (and even to operate these, since they were too complex for anyone else). Like Marie Rambert, she was flung in at the deep end; but she too was highly intelligent and musical, and succeeded brilliantly, making it possible for the choreographer to do things that would otherwise have been impossible.

Though the problems she faced were specially challenging, this was by no means the first time that a choreologist working at a choreographer's elbow had made a valuable contribution to the creation of a new work: such things had been happening for years in many different companies and countries. The success of such collaboration makes it possible to foresee a time when it will be the normal thing for choreographers to compose on paper, as dramatists and music composers have done for centuries: in fact company choreologists with creative gifts are already beginning to do this.

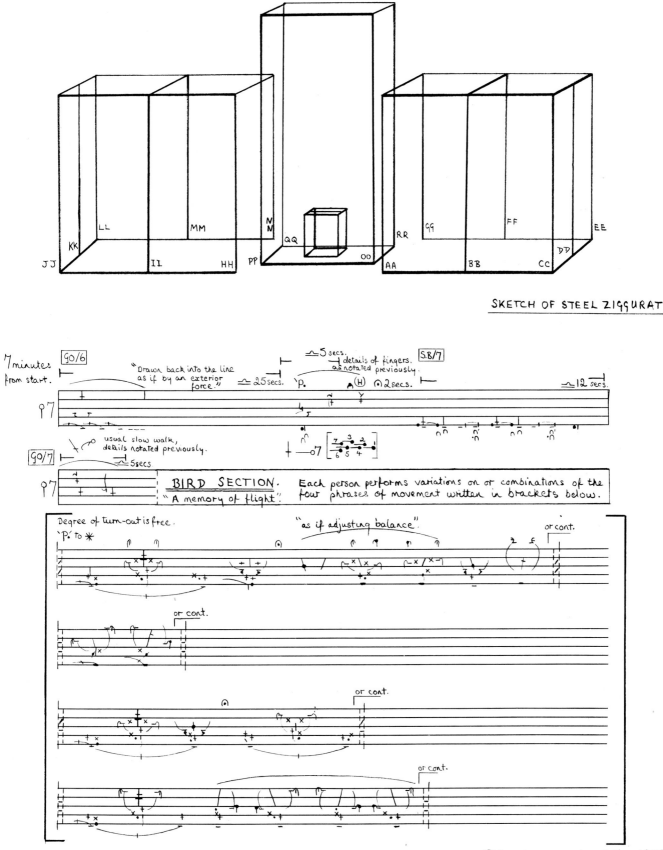

SKETCH OF STEEL ZIGGURAT

Acknowledgments

The photographs in this book were taken by Mike Davis with the exception of those provided by the Raymond Mander and Joe Mitchenson Theatre Collection (p. 10), and the Radio Times Hulton Picture Library (p. 11 and p. 13, bottom).

Index